The Teaching for Understanding Guide

The Teaching for Understanding Guide

Tina Blythe

and the Teachers and Researchers
of the
Teaching for Understanding Project

Jossey-Bass Publishers
San Francisco

Substantial discounts on bulk quantities of Jossey-Bass books are available to corporations, professional associations, and other organizations. For details and discount information, contact the special sales department at Jossey-Bass Inc., Publishers (415) 433-1740; Fax (800) 605-2665.

For sales outside the United States, please contact your local
Simon & Schuster International office.

Jossey-Bass Web address: http://www.josseybass.com

Manufactured in the United States of America.

Chapters Two and Three first appeared as "Putting Understanding Up Front" by David Perkins and Tina Blythe in *Educational Leadership*, Vol. 51, No. 5 (February 1994). Reprinted with permission of the Association for Supervision and Curriculum Development. Copyright © 1994 by ASCD. All rights reserved.

Interior design by Ralph L. Fowler.

Library of Congress Cataloging-in-Publication Data
Blythe, Tina, 1964–
    The teaching for understanding guide / Tina Blythe and the
teachers and researchers of the Teaching for Understanding Project.
    — 1st ed.
        p.   cm. — (The Jossey-Bass education series)
    ISBN 0-7879-0993-9 (paper)
    1. Teaching—Case studies.   2. Comprehension—Study and teaching—
Case studies.   3. Learning—Case studies.   4. Educational tests and
measurements—Case studies.   I. Title.   II. Series.
LB1025.3.B619   1998
371.102—dc21   97-33735

FIRST EDITION
PB Printing   10 9 8 7 6 5 4 3 2 1

Table of Contents

96026

List of Figures

Preface

Nurturing understanding is one of the loftiest aspirations of education and also one of the most elusive. The very concept of understanding raises a host of complex questions for thoughtful educators: What does it mean to understand something? How do students develop understanding? What things should they understand? How do we know how well they understand something? How can we consistently support the development of understanding?

In 1988, three faculty members at the Harvard Graduate School of Education—Howard Gardner, David Perkins, and Vito Perrone—began talking together about these questions. Realizing the importance and complexity of the issues surrounding understanding, they convened a group of school- and university-based colleagues who spent a year designing a five-year research project. The project mission was to develop a research-based, classroom-tested approach to teaching for understanding. With funding from the Spencer Foundation, the Teaching for Understanding Project was launched.

Over the course of the next five years, more than sixty school-based and thirty university-based educators and researchers contributed their time and expertise to defining understanding, identifying the aspects of classroom practice that best supported understanding, and wrestling with complex issues of assessing understanding. They conducted mini research projects that explored students' understanding of particular concepts and captured students' reflections on the process of developing understanding. Project members designed curriculum units, carried them out, and reflected together about what had worked and what hadn't.

From all of these efforts grew the Teaching for Understanding Framework, a tool for designing, conducting, and reflecting on classroom practices that nourish student understanding. Teachers (in both schools and universities) tried out the framework in their planning and teaching, shared their experiences, and recommended changes. As the framework reached final form, project members looked for ways to make it accessible to those who had not been directly involved in the project. Thus *The Teaching for Understanding Guide* was born.

Purpose and Audience

This book is a practical tool for making understanding a more achievable goal in classrooms. It is intended for teachers and administrators who want to add to their repertoire of resources and strategies for engaging students in meaningful and lasting learning experiences. It provides a full description of the Teaching for Understanding Framework and a sampling of planning ideas and aids that have been refined based on the experiences of the many teachers who have used this approach in their classrooms. Specific examples of curriculum pieces and classroom instruction, as well as the comments of teachers, show how the framework can be used in day-to-day practice. The sections within each chapter are intentionally short to facilitate the start-and-stop kind of reading that most teachers are forced by their busy schedules to do.

This book is not a kit, however. Teaching for understanding—like learning for understanding—is hard work, and there are no surefire recipes for success. Rather than offering answers, this book provides a tool (the framework) and examples to help teachers explore their own answers to questions such as these:

"What do I most want my students to understand?" "How does my current practice help them develop those understandings? What else could I try?" "How can I know how well my students understand what I am teaching?"

Rethinking one's classroom practice is a challenging process. This book will be most helpful to that process if reading it is accompanied by active engagement with the ideas presented in it, particularly if that engagement is supported by colleagues who are also interested in thinking and talking about understanding. The Reflection section at the end of each chapter suggests related activities, issues, and questions to facilitate further exploration of the chapter's ideas. These can be used individually (perhaps with the help of a journal) or in discussion with colleagues.

While this book grew out of an extensive research project, it does not contain a description of the research and development process. Those interested in this aspect of the Teaching for Understanding Project should see the companion to this book, *Teaching for Understanding: Linking Research with Practice*, edited by Martha Stone Wiske (Jossey-Bass, 1998). That volume provides a complete description of the collaboration between researchers and teachers in the project, the development of the framework, and its testing in classrooms.

Overview of the Contents

Chapter One provides a more detailed description of the various features of the book and its purposes. This chapter also offers some suggestions for how to use the book as a tool for self-reflection as well as for conversation with colleagues.

Chapter Two takes up several questions that are central to the enterprise of teaching for understanding: What is understanding? Why is it hard to teach for understanding? What helps students understand?

Chapter Three offers an overview of the Teaching for Understanding Framework. All four of the framework's elements are described through short definitions and brief examples.

Chapters Four through Seven each describe in detail one element of the framework. The chapters all begin with a brief introduction, which is followed by a detailed case study that portrays one teacher's efforts to use that piece of the framework in planning and teaching. Subsequent sections in each chapter include many shorter examples, general tips for planning and teaching, and answers to common questions asked about each framework element.

Chapter Eight explains a few general strategies for using the framework to plan a curriculum and carry it out in the classroom. It also provides some sample worksheets that teachers have found helpful in the planning process.

Chapter Nine answers the question, "How does the Teaching for Understanding Framework fit in with all the other new ideas I've heard about or used in my classroom?" This chapter characterizes briefly some of the terms, concepts, and strategies most often mentioned in conjunction with improving classroom practice and describes the degree to which this approach to teaching supplements or differs from them.

In the sidebars sprinkled throughout this book you will find quotations from teachers and students who have focused on teaching and learning for understanding. These quotations are intended to provide a sense of the different reactions, issues, concerns, and benefits that teachers and students in various contexts have experienced as they have put these ideas about teaching and learning for understanding into practice.

Four teachers—Eric Buchovecky, Lois Hetland, Bill Kendall, and Joan Soble—are quoted extensively. They are the teachers who worked most closely with researchers in piloting the version of the Teaching for Understanding Framework represented in this book. During the piloting process they reflected frequently, both informally and formally, on their experiences with using the framework's ideas in their practice. Their comments in this book are drawn from those reflections. Other quotations come from teachers who helped in early stages of the project to develop the framework or who encountered it in its fully developed form in a series of workshops (lasting from several days to several semesters). And some quotations come from teachers who read through earlier drafts of this book on their own, put its ideas into practice, and then reported their experiences either in discussions with the research staff or in writing.

It is not necessary to read this book from start to finish. It is designed to support browsing and selective sampling. Where concepts are discussed only briefly, comments in the margins will refer you to other places in the book that contain complete descriptions of them. Let your interest be your guide, and may your explorations of the Teaching for Understanding Framework prove fruitful!

Cambridge, Massachusetts   *Tina Blythe*
August 1997

The Authors

The teachers and researchers of the Teaching for Understanding Project represent diverse vantage points and a broad range of experience within the world of education. Some of us are university-based researchers and teachers; others are educators in elementary and secondary schools. While most of us work at the middle and high school level, we bring experiences from every grade level, from pre-K to graduate school. We have carried out our work in suburban and urban, public and private, and alternative and traditional settings.

We include novice educators and researchers and veterans of thirty-five years. Many of us have filled a variety of roles in the course of our careers: classroom teacher, school administrator, researcher, professional developer, curriculum designer. Our professional interests range from developmental and cognitive psychology to pre-service teacher education, from whole-school change to classroom instruction, and from educational technology to the structure and pedagogy of specific disciplines.

All of us believe that teaching for understanding is central to the education and lives of students. We hope that this book will provide a useful support to educators engaged in that important and challenging work.

A Note About Authorship

While I have served as the primary author of this book, the ideas contained in it are the work of many people. Those who made contributions to particular chapters are listed in those chapters.

Chapters Two and Three represent a collaborative coauthorship unlike that of the other chapters. These two chapters are a revised version of an article entitled "Putting Understanding Up Front" that David Perkins and I published in *Educational Leadership* in February 1994, with David Perkins as the senior author. The revised version is printed here with the permission of (and our gratitude to) the Association for Supervision and Curriculum Development.

The people listed as additional contributors in Chapters Four through Seven provided the inspiration for the case studies that appear in those chapters. As I point out in Chapter One, the case studies in this book are composites of two or more teachers' efforts, drawn together in order to portray succinctly the many different decision points and considerations that a teacher might face in working with each part of the framework. While these case studies do not portray exclusively the individual practice of the person or persons identified in the chapter header, the cases did benefit significantly from the expertise and experiences of these practitioners and researchers.

In the case of David Outerbridge (Chapter Five) and Dorothy Gould (Chapter Six), this inspiration came principally from researchers' observations of their classes, their recorded discussions with other teachers, and their own written reflections about their teaching and their use of the framework.

In Chapter Four, I drew from a curriculum unit developed by Veronica Boix Mansilla and Rosario Jaramillo. Their work was inspired by a unit developed and carried out by Phillip James. Similarly, a curriculum unit designed, carried out, and recorded by Eric Bondy and Bill Kendall served as the basis for the case study in Chapter Seven.

Acknowledgments

The Teaching for Understanding Guide has emerged from six years of conversation, research, experimentation, and collaboration on the part of the many researchers and teachers involved in the Teaching for Understanding Project. The book's production was the focus of one branch of a multifaceted operation. Since it benefited from the work carried out in each part of the project, special acknowledgment is due not only to the teachers and researchers who contributed directly to the development of this book but also to all of those involved in the project's various phases.

The Project

During the initial planning year of the Teaching for Understanding Project, many teachers opened their classrooms to researchers and gave their time generously for interviews and meetings. The work of Herb Baker, Neil Claffey, Roberta Dollase, Robyn Hallowell, Mary Halpin, Angela Johnson, Heidi Kaiter, Dick Maciel, Mary Ann Santos, Peg Schwartz, Rob Stark, and Bruce Ward provided the starting point for the subsequent five years of the project.

A number of teachers collaborated with the project in years two and three to help create the Teaching for Understanding

Framework—the heart of the project's efforts. They met with researchers and other teachers weekly, developed case studies of their classroom work, and challenged and refined the theory and language that eventually became the Teaching for Understanding Framework as it appears in this book. These teachers included Gayle Bartley, Wendy Bembery, Phyllis Bretholtz, David Bronson, Marshall Cohen, Jackie Cossentino, Joe Decelles, Sandy Dell, John DioDato, Gary Elliott, Dorothy Gonson, Dorothy Gould, Elizabeth Grady, Phillip James, Jim Johns, Ed Joyce, Alison Kenney-Hall, Socrates Lagios, Lyn Montague, Susan O'Brien, David Outerbridge, Steve Roderick, Brenda Scally, and Steven Smeed.

During the final stages of the project, several teachers worked closely with researchers to test and refine the framework. Eric Buchovecky, Lois Hetland, Bill Kendall, and Joan Soble devoted many hours to developing curriculum units with the framework, using those units in their classes, and reflecting on their experiences in writing and in conversation with researchers and one another. They and their students provided the bulk of the data on which the assessment of this framework was based.

In addition, several schools began to make use of the Teaching for Understanding Framework in the final years of the project: Wynn Middle School in Tewksbury, Massachusetts; the elementary, middle, and high schools of the ATLAS Communities project, especially Tanners Creek Elementary School, Rosemont Middle School, and Norview High School in Norfolk, Virginia; the Winchester (Massachusetts) Public Schools; teachers at Shady Hill School in Cambridge, Massachusetts; and a consortium of schools in Bogotá, Columbia. The experiences of the teachers and administrators in these schools provided important clues to the differences between whole-school and single-classroom use of the Teaching for Understanding Framework.

A number of researchers worked closely with teachers to develop and implement curricula, design the research methodology for exploring the effectiveness of the framework, collect data through interviews with teachers and students as well as classroom observations, and reflect on and solidify the project's theoretical underpinnings through discussion and writing. In these ways, Veronica Boix Mansilla, Eric Bondy, Anne Chase, Ada Beth Cutler, Roger Dempsey, Karen Hammerness, Elizabeth Hodder, Rosario Jaramillo, Peter Kugel, Catalina Laserna, Fiona Hughes-McDonnell, Barbara Neufeld, Judy Pace, Alexandra Rehak, Ron Ritchhart, Chris Unger, Noel White, and Daniel Wilson all contributed to one or more of the project's phases.

In addition to her involvement in the development of the framework, Joyce Conkling provided critical administrative support for all phases of the project. Matthew Woods filled her shoes during the final year. Their work was supported at various times by Wanda Bailey, Diane Downs, Cindy Kirby, Kathy Ivins, Sue Sebag, and Kathy Unger.

From inception to conclusion the Teaching for Understanding Project was guided by the thoughtful work of principal investigators Howard Gardner, David Perkins, and Vito Perrone and of project directors Rebecca Simmons and Martha Stone Wiske.

Book Development

The development of this book began in the third year of the project. We tried out, discarded, and revised many versions before settling on the current one. Roger Dempsey, David Perkins, Rebecca Simmons, Chris Unger, and Noel White all wrote initial pieces, from which the current work grew.

In addition, some teachers not otherwise connected with the project (though a few went on to become more involved) agreed to serve on one or more panels charged with the task of reading, critiquing, and attempting to plan curriculum units with various versions of the handbook. These panelists included Jim Crecco, John DioDato, Judith Evans, John Hayward, Jud Hill, Joanna Honig, Anita Honkonen, Joan Mountford, Yvonne Quinama, Joan Soble, Barbara Totherow, Linda Weber, and Lisa Weiss.

The student teachers of the Harvard Undergraduate Teacher Education Program (from 1992 to 1995), under the direction of

Elizabeth Hodder, provided additional feedback based on their readings and experiences as they worked toward their teaching certifications.

Many people from inside and outside the project read and provided detailed and insightful critiques of one or more of this book's later drafts. They included Gayle Bartley, Veronica Boix Mansilla, Eric Buchovecky, Marshall Cohen, Joyce Conkling, Jackie Cossentino, Roger Dempsey, Gary Elliott, Howard Gardner, Dorothy Gonson, Elizabeth Grady, Dee Gould, Elizabeth Hodder, Lois Hetland, Peter Kugel, Lyn Montague, David Outerbridge, David Perkins, Vito Perrone, Barbara Powell, Rebecca Simmons, Shari Tishman, Shirley Veenema, Noel White, and Martha Stone Wiske.

The final manuscript benefitted from the thoughtful advice of Lesley Iura and Christie Hakim at Jossey-Bass, the careful administrative work of Sara Hendren, and the unflagging support of Lyle Davidson, Thomas Hatch, and Steve Seidel.

Generous funding from the Spencer Foundation made all of this work possible.

T.M.B.

What This Guide Is (and Isn't) 1

Have you ever asked yourself these questions?

➤ "How do I decide what is most important for my students to learn?"

➤ "Can I convince others—and my own students—that what we are studying is important?"

➤ "What are my students really getting out of this class?"

➤ "Why can't my students seem to remember anything from the previous unit once we move on to the next one?"

➤ "Am I really reaching all my students?"

➤ "How can I make my class mean more to students than just another grade on their report card?"

➤ "How can I help students see that their grades aren't arbitrary?"

➤ "Will my students be able to use anything they learn in this class in the future? How will I know?"

> "How can I have a conversation with my colleagues about what we're teaching and what our students are learning?"

This book can help you answer them. It represents the collaborative thought and work of the teachers and researchers of the Teaching for Understanding Project, based at the Harvard Graduate School of Education. Over the course of five years, members of this group talked together, developed curricula, tried them out in classrooms, watched and talked with students, wrote case studies, and eventually solidified a framework that identifies the central aspects of planning and teaching for understanding.

Although they were developed principally with the help of middle and high school teachers and administrators, the ideas in this book have proven helpful to many elementary school teachers and administrators as well.

What This Guide Is

> "This approach feels very familiar. It describes the kind of teaching I already try to do in my class. For me it has become a tool for reflecting on and refining my teaching."
>
> **Jackie Cossentino, Eleventh- and Twelfth-Grade English Teacher, Cambridge, Mass.**

This book is a resource that provides useful ideas and practical strategies for teachers who want to give understanding a more consistently prominent place in their classrooms. In this book you will find

> A theory of understanding.

> A framework that lays out the essential ideas involved in teaching for understanding.

> Ideas for how to make understanding a more central and reachable goal in your classroom.

> Planning and teaching examples that draw on this framework.

> Criteria that you can use to reflect on and evaluate your efforts to plan and teach for understanding.

➤ Questions and activities that can help guide personal reflections and conversations with colleagues.

What This Guide Is Not

This book is not a script. Teaching for understanding is too complex an activity to be captured in easy steps or formulas. What this book offers is a framework to help you examine and shape your own classroom practice according to your goals, your particular teaching style, and your students' particular approaches to learning.

Neither is this book an exhaustive discussion of the research that either the members of the Teaching for Understanding Project or others have done. Above all else, the aim of this book is to provide useful and practical support for teachers—even given the limited time teachers have for reading and planning.

> For a description of the research that forms the basis of the Teaching for Understanding Framework, see *Teaching for Understanding: Linking Research with Practice*, edited by Martha Stone Wiske (San Francisco: Jossey-Bass, 1998).

Finally, this book is not an indictment of current teaching practice. Many ideas presented here are drawn from existing teaching practice. Much thoughtful work is already taking place in classrooms. One purpose of this book is to share these fine examples and to offer ways to sustain such practice over long periods of time.

About the Format

The pages of the book are divided into two columns: a section for the main text, and one for notes that will help your reading in several ways:

 Personal Perspective notes offer the reflections of teachers and administrators who have used the framework, as well as comments from the students in their classes.

Explanation notes accompany case studies and provide comments and generalizations about them.

 There's More notes supply cross-references to other sections of the book or other resources that offer more information about the topic.

> "Using this framework helped me to pull together a lot of approaches to planning and teaching that I intuitively felt were right. It has helped to provide direction and focus in my classroom."
>
> **Eric Buchovecky, Eleventh-Grade Physics Teacher, Belmont, Mass.**

At the close of each chapter is a Reflection section. It includes suggestions for applying the framework to your own practice and things to try either alone or with the group of colleagues with whom you are working.

About the Case Studies

Chapters Four through Seven include brief case studies to illustrate the process of planning and teaching for understanding. These cases are based on the work of teachers who used the approach described in this book. The cases are meant to be examples, rather than exemplars, since there is no one way to use this approach to teaching for understanding. In some instances these cases represent a composite of two or more teachers' efforts, drawn together in order to portray succinctly the variety of concerns and issues that can arise in dealing with any part of the framework. Therefore the names used in these cases are made up.

The four case studies as well as the numerous shorter examples that appear throughout the book are drawn from mathematics, science, English and language arts, and history and social studies; however, the approach described here has been used successfully with all subject areas and domains, including interdisciplinary work.

Suggestions for Enhancing the Book's Usefulness

The following suggestions will help you make the most of this book.

Browse through the book and begin with the chapters that interest you most. There is no prescribed order or linear process to this guide. Follow your own instincts in deciding where to start and how to continue. If you prefer to begin with an overview of the theory and the framework, read Chapters Two and Three first. If examples of practice are the best place to start, skip to the brief case studies that are the heart of Chapters Four through Seven. If you would rather begin by thinking about your own practice, concentrate on the Reflection sections at the end of each chapter and on Chapter Eight, which includes planning materials.

Let it serve your own work. Throughout this book you will find many examples of classroom practice that illustrate particular applications of the framework. However, the most useful examples will be the ones that you work out in your own mind and your own classroom, based on your experiences as a teacher. As you read and discuss the ideas in this book, try applying them directly to your own teaching and curriculum. You might think about units with which you are not entirely satisfied or with which you have become bored over time. Remember the concepts that your students typically have difficulty grasping. How might the key ideas of the Teaching for Understanding Framework be used to reshape or develop a new approach?

Try to find a group of colleagues to work with. It is certainly possible to work through this book on your own and to glean many useful ideas and techniques from it. However, many teachers have found it even more helpful to collaborate with colleagues in ongoing discussion groups that focus on the ideas contained in this book. In the process of using the Teaching for Understanding Framework you will find yourself engaged in many thought-provoking and challenging tasks: reexamining deep-seated assumptions and priorities that underlie your practice, developing and refining approaches to complex

> "It's difficult to have conversations about teaching and learning because, as teachers, we all come from such different perspectives. While this framework felt awkward at first—a little like learning a new language—I know that it has helped me to become clearer about what I mean when I'm talking with others about my teaching practice."
>
> **Bill Kendall, Ninth- and Tenth-Grade Algebra and Geometry Teacher, Braintree, Mass.**

topics, trying out new teaching strategies. Having colleagues to talk with can help in a number of ways:

1. Colleagues can serve as sounding boards and critical friends in the process of developing new ideas. Just as students need the input of peers and teachers (not just self-assessment) in order to evaluate their own learning, we as teachers need the input of our colleagues to assess and refine our own work.

> "On my own, I couldn't have rethought my curriculum as deeply or as thoroughly. I really needed someone to help me ask the big questions, to remind me of the things I forget."
>
> **Joan Soble, High School English Teacher, Cambridge, Mass.**

2. Negotiating central goals and standards for student work needs to be a community effort. Although we might have our own ideas about what things are most important for our students to understand, it is critical that we shape and hone these ideas in conversations with others—colleagues who teach at our grade level, those who teach at the levels below and above, those who are disciplinary or domain experts, parents, businesspeople, and other community members. The process of defining goals and standards produces no "right answers"; however, drawing on the expertise that others have to offer makes it more likely that the goals and standards we define will equip our students with the understanding they will need in the world beyond our classrooms.

3. Developing understanding is a difficult enterprise. The process of coming to understand our own teaching and our students' learning is no exception. We need the support and encouragement of colleagues who are engaged in similar efforts and with whom we can share our struggles and successes.

REFLECTION

This section contains suggestions that you might use to begin applying the ideas in this book to your own practice.

Getting Started

You might begin exploring the topic of teaching for understanding by browsing through this book. You might also want to share it with colleagues who you think might be interested in it. Is there a person (or a few people) who might want to meet regularly with you over the course of a few months to discuss and try out the Teaching for Understanding Framework?

Journal Writing

Many teachers who have worked with the Teaching for Understanding Framework have found it helpful to keep a journal of their thoughts. This is particularly helpful if you decide to work by yourself. The journal is a place where you can jot ideas, track the development of your thinking, and refine your curriculum plans. You could begin by writing about or discussing with your colleagues some the following questions:

> *As you browse through the book, what catches your eye? What intrigues you? What questions do you have?*

> *What do you hope to learn through the process of trying out the Teaching for Understanding Framework and talking about it with fellow teachers?*

Your notes on these questions might be useful in guiding your reading and planning as you work through the rest of the book.

Understanding
Understanding

with David Perkins

2

A mathematics teacher asks her students to design a floor plan

for a community center, including dance areas
and a place for a band. Why? Because such a
design will involve several geometric shapes
and a defined area, and the students must use

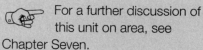
For a further discussion of this unit on area, see Chapter Seven.

what they have studied about the computation of area to make
an effective plan.

A history teacher asks his students to reflect
on and write about their experiences holding
jobs and their relationships with their employers. Why? Because the students will soon be

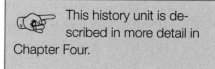
This history unit is de-scribed in more detail in Chapter Four.

studying the Industrial Revolution, focusing on how it shaped
the experiences of and relationships among members of various
social classes in the United States.

A science teacher asks her students to prepare statements explaining their position on whether the president should sign an
international environmental treaty. Why? Because preparing

these statements will engage the students in evaluating and applying a number of scientific perspectives on global warming.

Anyone alert to current trends in teaching practice will not be surprised by these examples. They illustrate the commitment on the part of many teachers to engage students more thoughtfully in the subject matter they are learning by helping students to draw connections between their lives and the subject matter, between principles and practice, past and present, and present and future.

Yet there is also something unusual about these examples: not what appears on the surface but what lies underneath it. These three learning activities were developed with the help of a simple set of guidelines called the Teaching for Understanding Framework.

"Teaching for understanding? What do you think I've been doing all these years!"

Alan Kidder, Fifth- and Sixth-Grade Teacher, Okinawa, Japan

Not that teaching for understanding is a new idea. Facilitating understanding is one of the most persistently honored goals of teaching. Virtually all teachers teach for understanding, among other things. We set goals for our students' understanding. We want our students to grasp the significance of the Declaration of Independence and how it fits into the tapestry of history. We want them to see the logic of the Pythagorean theorem. We want them to identify the complicated dilemmas in Macbeth and relate those dilemmas to their own lives.

To help them develop these understandings, we employ a number of strategies. We strive to explain clearly. We look for opportunities to clarify. We assign open-ended tasks such as planning an experiment or critiquing a book or debating an issue—tasks that call for and build understanding.

But helping students acquire understanding is difficult work. We commonly find that our students understand much less than we had hoped for. Students get confused by fractions and algebraic formulas; they miss the point of poems; they have trouble writing essays that show real understanding. Moreover, they usually do not see the connections between what they learn in school and what they do outside of school.

Research on students' understanding confirms the difficulty of the enterprise of teaching for understanding. A number of studies have documented students' misconceptions about key ideas in mathematics and the sciences (for instance, seeing evolution as progress toward ever-greater perfection); their parochial views of history (for example, thinking that living conditions in the past or in other cultures are like those they have experienced); their tendency to reduce complex literary works to stereotypes, and so on. Despite all of our efforts, student understanding still seems elusive. Why?

The Difficulty of Teaching for Understanding

Several factors appear to be at work. First, for most teachers, enhancing student understanding is only one of many agendas. Most of us distribute our efforts more or less evenly among that objective and a number of others (helping students develop self-esteem, for example). Second, the schools in which we work and the tests for which we prepare our students usually offer little support for teaching for understanding. Third, questions of strategy abound: what curricula, activities, and assessments will best support teaching for understanding, day in and day out?

In addressing the first two factors, all of us in education need to weigh carefully the importance of teaching for understanding. Not surprisingly, the Teaching for Understanding Project takes the position that understanding deserves special attention. This is not to deny the importance of other educational goals. For instance, a number of routine skills such as adding, spelling, and composing grammatically correct sentences certainly need to be stressed. But what use are students to make of the history or mathematics they learn unless they understand it? Among the agendas of education, surely understanding must rank far up on the short list of high priorities.

> "At first I thought, well of course I emphasize understanding. But then I started thinking about all the things I take into consideration when I give grades—effort, neatness, attendance, improvement, how the rest of the class did, whether or not the work was on time, whether or not they followed the right [format]. . . . Not that those things shouldn't matter, but it's surprising how much else besides understanding figures into it."
>
> **Joe Decelles, Ninth-Grade English Teacher, Boston, Mass.**

As to the matter of strategies, the Teaching for Understanding Project sought to develop an approach to planning and teaching that would help teachers answer the difficult question of how best to nurture students' understanding.

What Is Understanding?

At the heart of the Teaching for Understanding Framework lies a very basic question: What is understanding? Good answers to this question are not at all obvious. Consider the difference between understanding and knowing. We all have a reasonable conception of what knowing is: when a student knows something, he or she can bring it forth on demand—tell us the knowledge or demonstrate the skill. Understanding is a subtler matter. It goes beyond knowing, but how?

For a further discussion of the research underlying the work of the Teaching for Understanding Project, see *Teaching for Understanding: Linking Research with Practice*, edited by Martha Stone Wiske (San Francisco: Jossey-Bass, 1998).

To answer this question, the Teaching for Understanding Project formulated a view of understanding, called the performance perspective, that is consonant with both common sense and a number of sources in contemporary cognitive science. The performance perspective says, in brief, that understanding is a matter of being able to do a variety of thought-provoking things with a topic, such as explaining, finding evidence and examples, generalizing, applying, analogizing, and representing the topic in new ways.

For example, even if a student "knows" Newtonian physics to the extent that he or she can apply certain equations to routine textbook problems, we would not necessarily be convinced that the student *understands* it. But suppose the student can find examples of Newtonian physics at work in everyday experience. (Why do football linemen need to be so big? So that they will have high inertia.) Suppose the student can make predictions that illustrate Newtonian principles. (Imagine a bunch of astronauts in space having a snowball fight. What happens as they throw and get hit by snowballs?) The better the student can handle a variety of thought-provoking tasks concerning Newton's theories, the readier we would be to say that the student has developed an understanding of them.

The same is true in other disciplines. A student who has an understanding of the First Amendment can appreciate its relevance to current debates about the uses of the Internet and draw on that appreciation to build and counter arguments. A student who has developed her understanding of the power of imagery can select and critique various metaphors for the title of an essay. And so on.

It is important to bear in mind that the development of understanding is a continuous process. This idea can run counter to intuitive notions of understanding. We might say in everyday conversation with a friend, "Oh, *now* I understand!" Or when a student responds correctly to a question during class discussion, we might think to ourselves, "She finally gets it!" While certainly there are breakthroughs and epiphanies as we develop understanding, virtually no one reaches a point where he or she understands everything there is to understand about a particular topic: there are always more and more complex tasks to be completed, more and more applications and connections to be explored. However, for instructional purposes teachers usually do articulate an expectation for a particular level of understanding that they want all students to achieve for a given topic.

> "If I can get the whole—take all the information and put it together—then I understand. But if I don't say anything new about what I'm learning, then I don't understand."
>
> **Pat, Seventh-Grade Student, Cambridge, Mass.**

In summary, understanding is being able to carry out a variety of actions or "performances" that show one's grasp of a topic and at the same time advance it. It is being able to take knowledge and use it in new ways. In the Teaching for Understanding Framework, such performances are called "understanding performances" or "performances of understanding."

Is every student performance a performance of understanding? By no means. Although they can be immensely varied, by definition performances of understanding must take students *beyond* what they already know. Many student performances are too routine to be understanding performances: answering true-false quizzes, performing standard arithmetic exercises, and so on. Such routine performances have importance, too, but they do not build understanding.

It is important not to equate routine performances with small or brief performances of understanding. Although the term *performance* can sometimes carry the connotation of a lengthy, public display, a *performance of understanding* refers to any instance in which students use what they know in new ways. Thus finding two or three examples of chemical bonding in everyday experience is as much a performance of understanding for one student as creating new chemical bonds is for another, although certainly the two actions differ markedly in their complexity.

How Do Students Learn for Understanding?

How do you learn to roller-skate? Certainly not just by reading instructions and watching others, although these actions may help. Most centrally, you learn by skating—and if you are a good learner, by *thoughtful* skating: you pay attention to what you are doing, capitalize on your strengths, and work on your weaknesses.

"Instead of just going over it in class, it helps you more if you actually do it. Instead of saying 'This is how it's done,' if you actually go out and see how it works in real life, then you will understand more."

Paul, Tenth-Grade Student, Braintree, Mass.

It is the same with understanding. If understanding a topic means building up performances of understanding around that topic, then the mainstay of learning for understanding must be actually carrying out such performances. Learners must spend the larger part of their time with activities that ask them to do thought-provoking tasks such as explaining, making generalizations, and, ultimately, applying their understanding on their own. And they must do these things in a thoughtful way, with appropriate feedback to help them do better.

This agenda becomes urgent when we think about how youngsters can spend their classroom and homework time. Many school activities are not performances that build or demonstrate understanding; rather, they build knowledge or routine skills. Moreover, when students do tackle understanding performances such as interpreting a poem or designing an experiment, they may get little guidance about criteria, little feedback before the final product to help them make it better, and few occasions to reflect on their progress.

Even though we are all trying, we need to do more. To get the understanding we want, we need to put understanding up front. And that means putting thoughtful engagement in understanding performances up front.

REFLECTION

It can be helpful to think about understanding in a more personal way. Try reflecting on some things that you understand well. Think in broad terms: you can include things you learned in school, such as analyzing poetry or proving geometry theorems, but you might also want to include things you learned outside of school, such as gardening, carpentry, or raising children. You might then use the following questions to guide your journal writing or discussion with colleagues:

➤ *How do you know that you understand these things well?*

➤ *What helped you to develop that understanding?*

If you are working with others, try comparing notes and making some generalizations about the following points:

➤ *The kinds of things you understand well (for instance, some people notice that their list tends to include activities that they do frequently or activities that they particularly enjoy).*

➤ *What you take as evidence of your understanding (for example, being able to resolve new problems related to a topic is an*

ability that many people cite as evidence of their understand-
ing of the topic).

➤ *The things that helped you to develop that understanding (a*
close relationship with a mentor or a lot of hands-on practice
are two examples).

As a final step, you might try comparing your generalizations to
the performance view of understanding described in the chapter:

➤ *What are the similarities between your description of develop-*
ing understanding and the definition given in the chapter?

➤ *What are the differences?*

The Teaching for Understanding Framework

with David Perkins

Developing understanding means doing things—using old knowledge in new situations to solve novel problems. But what exactly do we want our students to understand? How do we help them develop these understandings? And how do we gauge their progress and provide them with feedback? The framework developed by the Teaching for Understanding Project provides a language for discussing and creating curricula that address these issues.

The Four Parts of the Framework

The framework includes four key ideas: generative topics, understanding goals, performances of understanding, and ongoing assessment. (Although the four parts of the framework are usually presented in this order, the ordering is somewhat arbitrary. You can begin your discussions or planning sessions with any part.)

Generative Topics

Not all topics (concepts, themes, theories, ideas, and so on) lend themselves equally to teaching for understanding. For instance, it is easier to teach statistics and probability for understanding than quadratic equations, because statistics and probability connect more readily to familiar contexts and other subject matters. If students need to develop an understanding of colonial tax policies, then the Boston Tea Party might be a good generative topic since it dramatizes in an interesting way the issues surrounding those policies. Generative topics have several key features: They are central to one or more disciplines or domains. They are interesting to students. They are accessible to students (there are lots of resources available to help students pursue the topic). There are multiple connections between them and students' experiences both in and out of school. And perhaps most important, they are interesting to the teacher.

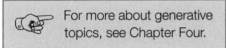 For more about generative topics, see Chapter Four.

Of course, one might argue that anything can be taught for understanding—even quadratic equations! It is just a matter of good teaching. This is true, but some topics are more central to a discipline or domain, more interesting to teachers, more accessible to students, and more easily connected to students' experiences than others. These topics should form the core of the curriculum.

However, many of us feel restricted to an established curriculum: particular topics must be taught regardless of whether they are generative or not. One solution is to give a topic a more generative cast by adding a theme or a perspective to it—for example, teaching *Oedipus Rex* as part of an exploration of family relationships or teaching about the food chain to illustrate that all living things are interconnected.

Understanding Goals

The trouble with generative topics is that they are almost too generative. Each topic offers the opportunity to develop many

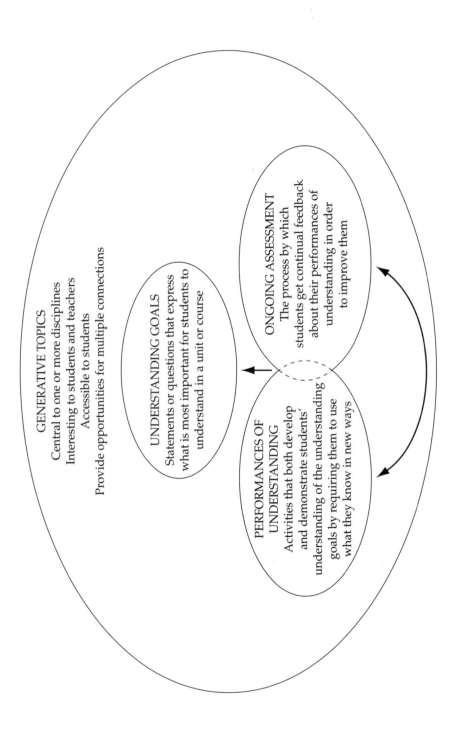

GENERATIVE TOPICS
Central to one or more disciplines
Interesting to students and teachers
Accessible to students
Provide opportunities for multiple connections

UNDERSTANDING GOALS
Statements or questions that express
what is most important for students to
understand in a unit or course

ONGOING ASSESSMENT
The process by which
students get continual feedback
about their performances of
understanding in order
to improve them

PERFORMANCES OF
UNDERSTANDING
Activities that both develop
and demonstrate students'
understanding of the understanding
goals by requiring them to use
what they know in new ways

FIGURE 3.1   *The Teaching for Understanding Framework*

different understandings. To create a focus, teachers have found it useful to identify a few specific understanding goals for a topic. Teachers have also found it helpful to state these goals both in sentence form ("Students will understand . . ." or "Students will appreciate . . .") and as open-ended questions that can be posed directly to students.

Suppose that the generative topic is "The Boston Tea Party as a Political Protest." One understanding goal for that topic might be "Students will understand the features that make the Boston Tea Party like and unlike other political protests of various historical periods." In question form, it might be phrased this way: "How is the Boston Tea Party similar to and different from other historical political protests, and why?" Another understanding goal might be "Students will appreciate the state of mind incited by deprivation of civil rights." The question form might be "What happens when people are deprived of their civil rights?" There is never a "right" list of understanding goals; the point is to lend focus to the ensuing instruction.

☞ Chapter Five presents a more detailed description of both unit-level and overarching understanding goals.

In addition to such unit-sized understanding goals, there are also year-long or overarching understanding goals, sometimes called "throughlines." Such goals describe the understandings that you feel are most important for students to take away from your class. There might be several throughlines for a course, and each of the individual units that make up the course will have understanding goals that relate closely to those overarching understanding goals or throughlines.

For example, one overarching understanding goal for an American History course might be "How do we find out the truth about things that happened a long time ago?" (In statement form it might read "Students will understand the various considerations and strategies historians use to interpret evidence about the past.") If the course includes a unit on the American Revolution, a related unit-level goal might be "Students will understand how to read and judge the reliability of primary sources about the American Revolution."

Making these throughlines explicit for students helps to ensure that they will stay focused on developing the most essential understandings. Discussing throughlines with students gives them opportunities to revisit those understandings over the course of several different generative topics as they move through the semester or year.

Performances of Understanding

As discussed in Chapter Two, performances of understanding are at the heart of developing understanding. Thus they need to be linked closely to understanding goals. Students should be engaged in performances that demonstrate and develop understanding from the beginning to the end of the unit or course.

> ☞ For further explanation and more examples of performances of understanding, see Chapter Six.

For example, a class might devote several weeks or even months to a generative topic. Throughout this time the students would engage in a variety of understanding performances (supported by appropriate information on the topic from texts and the teacher) as they work toward a few understanding goals. The initial performance of understanding probably would be relatively simple. In the Boston Tea Party unit, for example, students might begin by discussing political protests they have witnessed. They could then move to slightly more demanding tasks, such as explaining in their own words why the Sons of Liberty opted to throw the tea into the harbor and speculating about what might have happened if their protest had taken another form. Successive understanding performances would present students with progressively subtler (but still accessible) challenges. Ultimately students might develop some "culminating" performance of understanding, such as an exhibition or an extended essay (arguing, for example, that the media age has transformed the nature of political protests).

Ongoing Assessment

Traditionally assessment comes at the end of a lesson or unit and focuses on grading and accountability. These are important functions for many purposes, but they do not serve students' learning needs. To learn for understanding, students need criteria, feedback, and opportunities for reflection throughout the entire sequence of instruction. In the Teaching for Understanding Framework this process is called ongoing assessment.

☞ Chapter Seven contains a more detailed discussion of ongoing assessment.

Instances of assessment might involve feedback from the teacher, from peers, or from self-evaluations. Sometimes the teacher may provide assessment criteria, and sometimes he or she may engage students in developing them. While there are many reasonable approaches to ongoing assessment, these factors are constant: public criteria, regular feedback, and frequent reflection throughout the learning process.

In summary, the four concepts discussed in this chapter delineate the core elements of the Teaching for Understanding Framework. Of course, they do not address every condition that affects student understanding. Other factors, such as classroom structure and teacher-student relationships, play important roles as well. The framework is meant only as a guide, one that keeps the focus on understanding while allowing teachers room to design units and courses that suit their particular styles and priorities as practitioners.

"The framework is like an insurance policy for me. All of the key ideas are things I've always known are important for my students. They're things I've always tried to incorporate into my teaching. But it's hard to keep track of all of those pieces all of the time. Using the framework as a lens to look at my teaching gives me a systematic way of making sure I'm consistently integrating all of the important elements."

Lois Hetland, Seventh-Grade Humanities Teacher, Cambridge, Mass.

What's New Here?

"Isn't this basically about using good activities?" you might reasonably ask. Yes, it is about teaching with good activities—good activities *plus*. It is the *plus* that is the special contribution of this framework.

While most of us have always sought to teach with good activities, often those activities do not involve performances of understanding. For instance, a *Jeopardy*-style history quiz, an art activity consisting of drawing the Boston Tea Party, a follow-the-recipe-type science experiment—all can be engaging activities. But typically they do not press the learners to think well beyond what they already know. While some of us often involve students in understanding performances, our curricula may lack the focus provided by thinking in terms of carefully selected generative topics and goals for understanding. Or some students may not receive the ongoing assessment needed to help them learn from their performances of understanding.

Many of the teachers who have collaborated with the Teaching for Understanding Project already do much, or even most, of what the framework advocates. They have described the framework as useful because it provides a language with which to discuss classroom practice with other teachers. It helps them sharpen the focus of their efforts. Since the framework grew out of teachers' practice, it would be odd if the kind of teaching it advocated were to come as a surprise to most teachers. Instead, it should look familiar: "Yes, that's the kind of teaching I like to do—and sometimes, even often, the kind I do." We already strive to teach for understanding. So this performance-based view of teaching for understanding does not aim at radical, burn-the-bridges innovations. Its banner is not "completely new and wholly different" but a just-as-crucial "more and better."

> "The framework is a representation of what good teaching is. It captures what good teachers do so that we can take gut feelings and make them more explicit and visible."
>
> **Meryl Launer, Seventh-Grade Teacher, Norwalk, Conn.**

REFLECTION

To begin thinking in more concrete terms about the framework, you might reflect on a topic or unit you teach that you feel your students understand well. Here are some questions that could guide your reflection and discussion with colleagues:

> ➤ *What do your students come to understand well?*

> ➤ *How do you know?*

➤ *What helps them develop that understanding?*

Consider, too, a unit in which you were not convinced that your students understood what you had hoped they would. How did the approach you took in teaching that unit differ from the approach you took for the one you just described?

If you are working with a group, try drawing some generalizations across your reflections:

➤ *What kinds of things do your students come to understand?*

➤ *What do you take as evidence of your students' understanding?*

➤ *What does and does not help them to develop that understanding?*

Try looking back at the generalizations you made at the end of Chapter Two and compare that list with this one. How are your own most powerful learning experiences like and unlike the experiences your students have in your classroom?

You might also compare the units you described in this Reflection with the framework:

➤ *In what ways is your approach similar to the framework's?*

➤ *Are there ways in which the framework and your approach differ?*

➤ *Do the differences suggest modifications you might want to make, either to your practice or to the framework?*

Generative
Topics

4

with Veronica Boix Mansilla, Phillip James, and Rosario Jaramillo

Determining what material to teach in a course can be one of the most challenging tasks a teacher faces. Our students have so much to learn—and so little class time in which to begin to learn it. How do we make decisions about what to include in a course? What material is going to be the most fruitful? In teaching for understanding, the answer is "generative topics."

Generative topics are issues, themes, concepts, ideas, and so on that provide enough depth, significance, connections, and variety of perspective to support students' development of powerful understandings. The following case study describes one teacher's efforts to identify and develop such a topic.

Case Study: Finding Generativity in a History Unit

As Paul reflected on the Teaching for Understanding Framework, he was most intrigued by the idea of generative topics. As an eleventh-grade advanced placement American history teacher, he had an established list of topics that he needed to cover with his students over the course of the year. Yet Paul was also concerned about his students' understanding. While his students amassed large quantities of facts, they had difficulty making sense of them. Their essays often lacked depth, both in terms of insight and in terms of the evidence they presented. His students seldom invoked events or issues that had been discussed prior to the unit in which they were currently engaged, even when such references would help to make their arguments stronger.

Paul presented his concern to his colleagues in the teaching for understanding discussion group to which he belonged. With the group's encouragement he decided to spend some time developing a generative topic. He chose to begin with the Industrial Revolution. It was a topic he remembered studying with relish in college; yet he was always a little disappointed with the flat-footedness of his students' march through coal mines, labor strikes, and urbanization.

As a group, the teachers created an "idea web" around the topic of Industrial Revolution (see Figure 4.1). After ten minutes of brainstorming, it was clear that the greatest concentration of associations were clustered around the idea of progress. Another history teacher in the group pointed out that if Paul could help his students to question the notion of progress, he would be engaging them in a debate central to the work of many historians. At the same time he would be helping them conquer one of the most prevalent misconceptions adolescents hold about history: that with every passing year, human beings are better off than those who came before.

Paul himself felt most drawn to the social history aspects of the topic: For whom did the Industrial Revolution represent progress, and in what respects? For whom was it damaging?

> For Paul, developing a generative topic is the most powerful starting place for working with the framework. Other teachers, however, may choose to begin with understanding goals, performances of understanding, or ongoing assessment.

> Creating an idea web is a technique teachers often use to explore the generativity of a particular topic. It is a method of brainstorming that allows you both to generate a lot of ideas quickly and to map the relationships among those ideas. The parts of the idea web that are especially thick with connections are usually good bets for yielding generative topics (see "progress" on Figure 4.1).

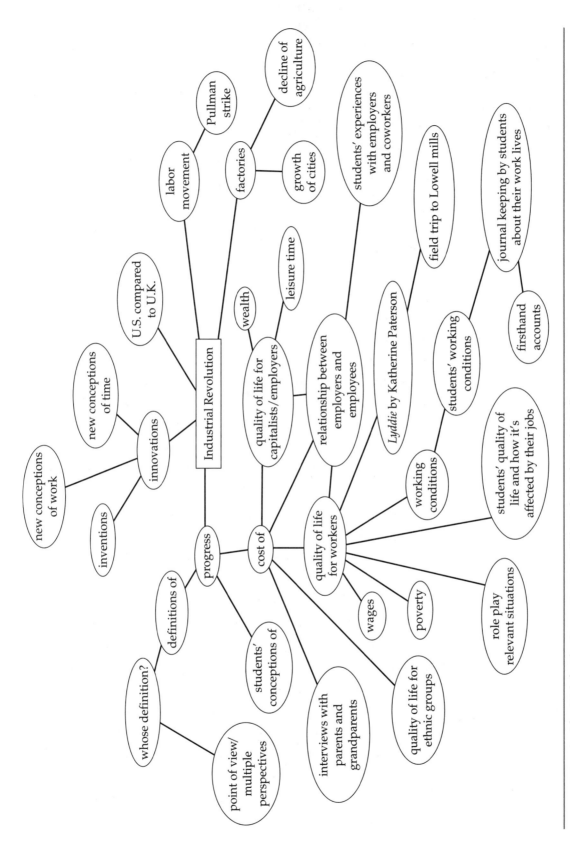

FIGURE 4.1   *An Idea Web for the Generative Topic "The Industrial Revolution"*

What were the long-and short-term gains and losses for various social classes and ethnic groups?

From his years of experience he knew that most of his students would associate the Industrial Revolution with the proliferation of machines. He searched the idea web for ideas about other, more personal links that would help his students focus on the societal changes of the times. He hit on one: he knew from the before-the-bell chatter in his classroom that many of his students were working in part-time jobs, some for the first time. Those experiences would give them some inkling of the employer-employee relationships that developed during the Industrial Revolution. Also, focusing on employers and employees would give Paul and his students a way into the social history of the topic by highlighting the huge gulf between the way those two classes experienced the Industrial Revolution.

Paul also remembered his class's lively discussions about gender issues, a topic the students themselves frequently introduced. Comparing the effects of the Industrial Revolution on women and men would be another way to help students broaden their perspectives.

Paul titled his unit "What Do We Mean by 'Progress'?" On the first day of class he asked his students to write a brief paper addressing the following questions: "In what ways does the Industrial Revolution represent progress to you? In what ways does it not?" Paul then collected the papers to hold until the end of the unit, when students could use them to assess the development of their understanding.

Paul launched the first discussion of the unit by opening up the issue that would tap his students' personal interest in the topic. He asked the class members to talk about a job they had held: What was the job? What was rewarding about the work?

> "Progress" is beginning to look like a good bet as a generative topic for two reasons: first, Paul is interested in it (the best generative topics are ones that deeply interest the teacher); second, it is an issue that is central to the discipline being taught (in this case, history). Both of these characteristics are important to a generative topic.

> For more ideas about planning with the framework, see Chapter Eight.

> By asking about his students' jobs, Paul is satisfying two important criteria of generativity: engaging his students' interest and allowing them to make connections to their personal experiences.

The Teaching for Understanding Guide

What made it difficult? Who did they work for? What was their relationship with that person? How did they feel about their employer, and why?

Then, to encourage his students to think about that relationship historically, Paul asked them about their parents' experiences with work, and their grandparents'. Were their grandmothers' experiences different from their grandfathers'? How had the employer-employee relationship changed over time? Where would they go to find out? Who could they ask?

Over the course of two weeks, students wrote about their own work experiences and conducted informal interviews with family members, which they shared in class discussion. They discussed primary sources from the Industrial Revolution era that portrayed employers' and employees' points of view about the quality of their lives. They debated whether or not the change in women's roles represented progress for them economically and socially. They also analyzed their textbook's description of the Industrial Revolution for evidence of the author's definition of progress. Finally, Paul asked them to revise their initial papers in light of the work they had done.

> ☞ These activities are examples of performances of understanding. For a further description of this piece of the framework, see Chapter Six.

Key Features of Generative Topics

Generative topics are central to one or more domains or disciplines. Issues that foster understanding allow students to gain the necessary skills and understanding to proceed successfully to more sophisticated work in the domain or discipline. Typically such issues are also of interest to professionals in the field.

Generative topics are interesting to students. The generativity of a topic varies with the age, social and cultural contexts, personal interests, and intellectual experiences of students.

> ✍ "This kind of learning [for understanding] is very different—not like straight information with right and wrong answers to things. This is loose, in a way, but it helps by centering us around something like a theme. . . . You can relate back to the theme. You can connect things to it."
>
> **Mark, Seventh-Grade Student, Cambridge, Mass.**

Generative topics are interesting to the teacher. Their teacher's passion for and curiosity about a particular issue or question will serve as the best model for students who are just learning how to explore the unfamiliar and complex territory of open-ended questions.

Generative topics are accessible. Accessibility in this case means that lots of age-appropriate resources are available to investigate the topic and that it can be addressed through a variety of strategies and activities that will help students with various strengths and inclinations make sense of it.

Generative topics offer opportunities for multiple connections. They give students the chance to make connections to their previous experiences, both in and out of school. They have an inexhaustible quality: they can always be explored more and more deeply.

Other Examples of Generative Topics

➤ *In biology:* the definition of life, rain forests, dinosaurs, endangered species, global warming.

➤ *In mathematics:* the concept of zero, patterns, equality, representations in signs and symbols, size and scale.

➤ *In history:* maritime disasters, survival, revolution, conflict, power.

➤ *In literature:* interpreting texts, folktales, humor, multiple perspectives.

Things That Are Not Necessarily Generative

"I have a lot of material to cover in my classes and 120 students to cover it with. I believe in spending more time on some topics than others, but I haven't got a lot of time to spend, so I pick those topics very carefully."

Marshall Cohen, Tenth-Grade Social Studies Teacher, Newton, Mass.

Generativity is as much a function of the way a topic is taught as it is of the topic itself or of students' interest in it. The most fascinating topics might well lose their productive capacity if reduced to a series of didactic questions with straightforward answers. Conversely, in the hands of a master teacher the most apparently insignificant topic can become generative. However, given the usual limits on teachers' time for planning and instruction, generativity might be most effectively engineered by looking for "best bets": topics important to one or more disciplines that also engage a particular group of students.

Planning Generative Topics

A first step in planning generative topics is to brainstorm ideas, preferably with colleagues. Think about what interests you most. Think about topics that have sparked your students' interest in the past.

Once you have identified ideas that seem particularly promising, create idea webs around them. Let your thinking range

 See Figure 4.1 for a sample idea web.

broadly: consider concepts, projects, resources, connections, and so on. Webbing is an opportunity to be adventurous. The ideas in the web can be refined later as you sort out what's most important.

Next, make selections from the idea web. Focus on those sections of the idea web that have the thickest nests of connections. Look for topics that are steeped in controversy, that are open to consideration from many different perspectives, that don't lend themselves to "right" answers, and that require students to formulate their own opinions.

Consult with other teachers, with friends, or with community members knowledgeable in the domain that you are teaching. Ask them what they think the "big ideas" are in that domain or discipline.

"The people who need to find a topic . . . generative should be . . . my students. I have to ask them the essential questions. I want to know what excited them to think about an idea in a new way. What lessons or subjects opened up their thinking, allowed them to experience the world with a slightly different perspective, enabled them to relate to someone or understand someone or something with greater insight or compassion? The question must be put to them."

Phyllis Bretholtz, Eleventh- and Twelfth-Grade Composition Teacher, Cambridge, Mass.

Teaching with Generative Topics

An important step toward making generative topics part of your teaching practice is to get to know your students. What are their likes and dislikes? What issues (in the news, in their personal lives, in their other classes) spark their interest? Are there any topics about which they hold strong opinions or enjoy arguing?

Early in the unit, you might also ask your students to create their own webs around the topic. Notice where their "connection concentrations" are. What new angles, issues, or perspectives do their idea webs suggest?

Finally, it is important to give your students time. No topic can be generative if your students do not have enough time to explore the material, make connections, and develop their understanding. Students should be allowed the time they need to explore essential content rather than covering large blocks of less generative material.

> "[My teacher] takes things at a more leisurely pace. . . . But it's not like he's not doing his job! He is going slower so if there are certain concepts that we couldn't understand, we could take the time to. He took the time to make sure that everybody understood. Sometimes other teachers go on to other subjects even if the students don't understand. Last year we did the heart on Tuesday, the digestive tract on Wednesday, and the circulatory system on Thursday. And if I couldn't keep up, I got lost."
>
> **Matt, Eleventh-Grade Student, Belmont, Mass.**

Common Questions About Generative Topics

Is teaching with generative topics the same as thematic teaching?

It can be, if the themes you choose to focus on are accessible to students, central to a domain or discipline, and have connections to students' experiences both in and out of school. One key difference is that thematic approaches to teaching tend to be interdisciplinary, but generative topics can be approached either across disciplines or through a single discipline.

How can I transform a set of topics that must be taught into generative topics?

Some teachers try putting a new spin on an old topic, as Paul does in the case study. For instance, ponds, cells, or the desert—typical topics for biology and general science classes—might be taught as part of a unit on interdependence.

REFLECTION

As you think about your own teaching, you might want to note the answers to some of the following questions in your journal:

> ➤ Which topics that you have taught strike you as being the most generative? What makes you think so?

> ➤ Which topics did your students find most interesting? (If you don't know, ask them!) Which did they find least interesting?

> ➤ Which topics did you find most interesting? Which were least interesting?

These notes could be useful in future planning sessions.

As you think ahead to the curriculum you will be teaching in the next few weeks, you might select one or two topics and, with your colleagues, create a web of ideas around them. (Again, notes on these questions might come in handy in future planning sessions.) Then consider these questions:

> ➤ What new connections or associations emerged as you brainstormed and created the idea web?

> ➤ Where are the "thick" parts of the web? Can you use them to put a new, generative spin on an old topic?

"My assigned topic for the year is 'Colonial America.' In thinking about how to make it generative, I ask myself a lot of questions: how will students be able to connect the ideas to their own lives, their own questions and plans, their dreams and interests?. . . I see opportunities in the literature, with numerous children protagonists, and in issues that concern young people today, such as maturity, independence, fairness, hypocrisy, following one's dreams, boredom, manipulation, peer pressure, fear, and bravery. I see opportunities for comparison with their own lives: How were children educated? What were their games and entertainments? How did they gain access to adult society? How did their daily lives compare to ours? I also ask what of substance can be understood through the various disciplines—particularly history, English, and geography, since those are my mandated subjects."

Lois Hetland, Seventh-Grade Humanities Teacher, Cambridge, Mass.

➤ *In what ways is the emerging generative topic interesting to you? How might it be interesting to your students?*

➤ *Does the topic seem important to the domain or discipline?*

If you and your colleagues are not sure about the answer to the last question, where might you go to find out? Some resources that you might consider include teachers in your school or other schools, district resource people, reference books or textbooks, professionals in the community who work in fields related to the discipline or domain, and teachers at local colleges and universities.

Picking out a few promising topics and keeping them in mind as you read through subsequent chapters might be a useful base for developing future units.

Understanding Goals

with David Outerbridge

5

Few of us would set off on a trip without first having a sense of where we want to go. The idea of wandering aimlessly might sound adventuresome or blissfully unpressured, but the fact is, we usually don't have unlimited money and vacation time. Because our resources are limited, we want to use them wisely. So we think carefully about where we'd like to go, and we have that destination in mind when we set out. Knowing where we want to end up helps us gauge our progress as we travel. It helps us decide when to stop to rest, when to forge ahead, and when to modify our itinerary.

Similarly, at the start of each unit we set off with our students on an intellectual journey, to explore the "territory" of a generative topic. Given that there are often lots of interesting points to explore, we might simply let our students follow their interests and roam where they will. But our time is very limited. We want to give our students time to explore what intrigues them, *and* we want to make sure they visit the important sites they might miss without guidance. Fortunately these territories are not wholly uncharted: experts in the various disciplines and domains we teach, our personal experiences, and our work with previous classes can help us to map out the landscape and pinpoint some of the most interesting and fruitful places to stop. So some parts of the journey we can leave to independent exploration, but in other parts we guide students to a few destinations that we want to make sure they reach.

In the Teaching for Understanding Framework, these destinations are known as understanding goals. They are the concepts, processes, and skills that we most want our students to understand. They help to create focus by stating where students are going.

Understanding goals come in two "sizes": unit-long and course-long. Unit-long understanding goals describe what we want students to get out of their work with a particular generative topic. Course-long understanding goals, known as overarching understanding goals, or throughlines, specify what we want our students to get out of their work with us over the course of a semester or year. As the following case study illustrates, both kinds of goals are usually phrased both as statements and as questions.

Case Study: Creating Unit and Course Understanding Goals in an English Class

In this case study, Jack, an English teacher, develops understanding goals first for a particular unit and then for his year-long course.

Part One: Identifying Understanding Goals for the Romeo and Juliet *Unit*

Jack, like Paul in Chapter Four, begins by reworking a unit with which he is dissatisfied. Other teachers prefer to use the framework to develop new units from scratch.

Jack estimated that this might be the fifteenth time he would "do" *Romeo and Juliet* in his twenty years of teaching high school English. The play was required reading for tenth graders in the lowest tier of the carefully tracked high school where Jack taught.

The Teaching for Understanding Guide

He easily could have repeated the unit without much planning or reflection, but something about his students' past experiences with the play had left him dissatisfied.

"Things go well enough in the beginning," Jack explained to his colleagues in the teaching for understanding discussion group to which he belonged, "but they seem to dribble off at the end. We read an act, and we discuss it. Then we read the next act and discuss it. And when we get through all of the acts, the kids write their papers, and we go on to the next piece of literature. But there's no real sense of closure, no sense that they really understood something from reading it." What he wanted this time around, he explained, was "some way to pull the whole experience together for them." His search for a clearer focus and a sense of closure for his students led Jack to concentrate on articulating understanding goals for the unit.

> Jack's concern about adding focus to the unit leads him to begin his planning process with unit-long understanding goals: articulating those concepts, skills, and ideas that are most important for his students to understand in the context of the unit. Someone else might have chosen to begin "tightening up" the unit by reshaping the performances of understanding so that they all focused students' attention on a few core issues. Another beginning point might have been to try framing the topic more generatively (as Paul does in Chapter Four).

As he reflected on his past experiences, he realized that his goals had always been broad and general: he wanted his students to understand what happens in the play and to understand the value of reading Shakespeare ("so maybe in next year's class they won't groan, 'Oh *no, Shakes*peare!' quite so loudly!").

In his weekly meeting with other teachers using the Teaching for Understanding Framework, Jack asked the group members to critique his understanding goals. "What do you mean by 'understand what happens'?" asked one teacher. She continued, "When kids talk about what happened, they can say, 'Juliet stands on her balcony

> Group members are urging Jack to make sure that his understanding goals for the play stated clearly what he feels is most important for his students to understand about it. This is the critical characteristic of understanding goals.

and talks about Romeo' or they can say, 'She wonders about the nature of identity.'" Another group member probed Jack's personal experiences as a reader: "How do *you* read *Romeo and*

Juliet? What do you get out it? Why is reading Shakespeare important to you?"

After a lengthy discussion of these issues and a few more revisions, Jack came up with the following list of unit-long understanding goals:

1. Students will understand that language shapes how the characters in *Romeo and Juliet* think and feel. (How does the language the characters use help us understand who they are?)

2. Students will appreciate the power of the poetry in the play. (Why would anyone bother to write a play in verse?)

3. Students will appreciate the careful sequencing of events in the plot that help to build up the dramatic tension. (How does Shakespeare create tension and interest in the play?)

4. Students will understand how to develop their own interpretation of the play and how to use evidence from the play to convince others of the validity of that interpretation. (What is my interpretation of the play, and how do I use evidence to defend it?)

As Jack reflected on these goals, particularly the last one, he realized why students' final papers on *Romeo and Juliet* had always left him dissatisfied. What he had really wanted was for students to come up with their own interpretations—and yet he had always assigned them a topic to write on. He also saw that he could spend more time helping students to understand what constituted a convincing use of evidence.

Ideas for other performances of understanding emerged as he studied his goals. In addition to having discussions on the issue of language, perhaps students could write about an important personal experience; by writing first in plain language and then in metaphorical language, they could compare the vividness and nuances of the two accounts. This performance would help them achieve the first understanding goal. They could also write a short essay comparing a few of the speeches given by different characters. Who uses rich and poetic language, and under what circumstances? Who doesn't? Why would the quality of the language and poetry vary so greatly? He brainstormed other ideas for performances of understanding that would help his students achieve the other understanding goals.

On the first day of the unit, Jack posted the question forms of the unit-long understanding goals in the classroom. His students seemed puzzled by some of them. When Jack asked them to jot down a few notes about how they might answer these questions given what they already understood, many of the students left several spaces blank. Making a mental note of the goals that seemed most difficult for them, Jack launched the students into reading and then discussing the language of the first scene. The students, unused to having to think about goals, were happy to follow his lead back to more familiar activities.

Several scenes later, Jack realized that the class seemed most interested in the family relationships and the effect they were having on Romeo and Juliet: Why would Juliet submit to a loveless marriage with Paris just because her father wanted her to? Why did the parents' prejudices have to have such adverse effects on their children?

He decided to invite his students into the process of establishing goals. He pointed to the goals already posted and asked the class to come up with a similar understanding goal that would capture what they wanted to understand about the

> Making the goals public to students is an important piece of the teaching for understanding process. Students need to know where they are headed if we ever want them to be able to get there without our having to do all the driving. However, students do not always grasp understanding goals when they first hear them. In fact, if they do understand them easily, there's a good chance that the goals might need to be more ambitious.

families in the play. After some debate the students offered, "We want to understand why the families make it so hard for Romeo and Juliet." After further discussion with Jack, they reformulated the goal into this question: "How do the family relationships contribute to making the play a tragedy?"

Jack asked the students what they might do to help them understand that issue better. One student, thinking about the process they had been using to study the language of the play, suggested that they find the places in the play where family members were interacting and analyze those sections carefully. Another suggested that they might think about difficult times in their own families and what had caused them. Jack collected a few more suggestions and used them to rework his plan for performances of understanding that students would carry out over the subsequent three weeks of reading the play.

Part Two: Identifying Overarching Understanding Goals for the Course

> Overarching understanding goals, or throughlines, describe the most important understandings that students should develop during an entire course. The understanding goals for particular units should be closely related to one or more of the overarching understanding goals for the course.

After Jack had planned and carried out a few units using the framework, he turned his attention to the overall design of his course. He had been fairly satisfied with the degree of focus developing within the units, but making the move from unit to unit still seemed a bit bumpy. To give his course more coherence, he began to identify and write down his overarching understanding goals, or throughlines.

Jack noticed that several understanding goals had remained constant through many of his units. He could recognize them even in some of the units he hadn't planned with the help of the framework. They were, in statement form, as follows:

1. Students will develop their understanding of what constitutes a good interpretation versus a shallow or incomplete one.

2. Students will develop their understanding of how to create a personal interpretation of a text and how to defend that interpretation by using evidence effectively.

3. Students will develop their understanding of how to argue for that interpretation in clear and coherent prose.

Since overarching understanding goals relate to every unit and generative topic in a course, Jack's approach is usually a good way to begin identifying them: once you have carried out several units, look for goals that sound similar and that appear in more than one or two units. You might also begin by writing down at the beginning of the semester the most important things you want your students to get out of your class—but plan to revisit and revise the list during the year.

A few goals seemed to pertain to only a unit or two (for example, wanting students to appreciate the richness of the poetic language in *Romeo and Juliet* or to understand how devices like foreshadowing help build dramatic tension in *Go Tell It On the Mountain*). These, Jack knew, were probably unit-level goals and not good candidates for overarching understanding goals.

Reviewing his list, he felt that it captured some important aspects of the course, but not all of them. He took the list to his teaching for understanding discussion group and asked for help. The group looked at the throughlines he had generated and then suggested others based on what they had heard him talk about during the weekly meetings. One group member asked, "What about the question you always ask us: why does anyone read literature to begin with?" Jack realized that even though this was a very important question

As with unit-long understanding goals, it often takes several rounds of revisions to develop a good list of throughlines. However, unlike unit understanding goals, throughlines need to capture the essence of a whole course. Throughlines often are rooted in deeply held but rarely articulated beliefs and values about both the subject matter and the teaching and learning processes. Therefore they often take longer to develop and refine than unit-long understanding goals—sometimes even several years.

to him personally, he had never raised it with his students. After some discussion with the group, he added it to his list. It was, after all, the question that interested him the most, as well as the one that really undergirded the whole course. If his students didn't understand why it was important to read and write about literature, then why would they care about any of the other goals on his list?

Another group member asked, "Isn't your course organized around genres—first short stories, then novels, then plays? Is there anything important about the qualities of the various genres that you want your students to understand?" Jack said that it was important to him for his students to compare the genres, but he admitted that time was often so short at the close of units that he either forgot or decided to forgo asking students to think back to previous units in order to make comparisons. His colleague suggested that adding such an overarching understanding goal might help him to give the development of that understanding more prominence in the course. Jack agreed.

Several weeks into the second semester, after making further revisions to his list of throughlines, Jack posted it for his students. He explained to them that these were the goals he felt it was most important for them to understand as a result of their work in the class. He also told

> As with unit-long understanding goals, it is essential to tell your students your overarching understanding goals.

them that he was still working on the list and invited their comments and feedback on it. "What about writing complete sentences? You're always telling us to do that," suggested one student. "Or how about developing our personal writing process? That's another thing you tell us a lot," suggested another.

To the first student Jack responded that understanding how to write complete sentences was really a part of the third overarching understanding goal—understanding how to argue for a particular interpretation of a work using clear and coherent prose. But the second student had a point, he mused. Jack felt strongly that no single approach to writing worked well for everyone. As a result he usually tried to encourage students to experiment with new approaches to writing—different ways of generating ideas and different techniques for organizing and developing them. He acknowledged to his students that understanding their own best approach to writing might indeed be an important overarching understanding goal.

After further discussion, Jack and his students converted the list of overarching understanding goals into question form:

1. Why do people read literature? What do I get out of reading literature?

2. What are the similarities and differences between genres? Why would someone choose to read or write in one genre rather than another?

3. What makes an interpretation a good one?

4. How can I develop a personal interpretation of a text and defend it with evidence?

5. How can I convey my interpretation in clear and coherent prose?

6. What approach to writing works best for me?

> Overarching understanding goals, like unit-long understanding goals, can address a variety of understandings. Some of Jack's understanding goals have to do with mastering processes and skills (developing an interpretation and writing about it convincingly), some deal with the substance of the discipline itself (understanding differences and similarities among genres), and some concern students' finding their personal connections to the domain or the discipline (learning what they get from reading literature and refining their own approach to writing).

Once he and his students had put the goals in question form, Jack began to use them in class in a variety of ways. He began by asking his students to write down their responses to each of the questions while reflecting on the work they had done in the first semester. He did this twice more over the course of the second semester, compar-

> Overarching understanding goals (throughlines) can be a valuable teaching tool. They help students see the purposes that underlie their daily work, make connections among various topics and assignments, and track their own developing understandings.

ing later responses to earlier ones, as one way of checking students' developing understandings. At the beginning of each unit he talked with his students about how the unit understanding goals related to the larger, overarching understanding goals.

With each assignment he asked his students to identify the goals they would be working toward. He encouraged them to review previous assignments that had addressed the same goals and to draw on what they had already learned in order to carry out their current work.

Key Features of Understanding Goals

Understanding goals identify the concepts, processes, and skills that we most want our students to understand. They are worded in two ways: as statements (in forms such as, "Students will understand . . ." or "Students will appreciate . . ." or "Students will develop their understanding of . . .") and as open-ended questions ("What are the important similarities and differences among different genres in literature?").

There are two "sizes" of understanding goals: fairly specific, unit-long understanding goals and broader, overarching understanding goals, or throughlines. Unit-long understanding goals express what you believe to be most important for your students to learn from a unit. Throughlines express what you think is most important for your students to understand from the entire course.

Unit-long understanding goals focus on the central aspects of a generative topic. Overarching understanding goals span topics: they can be addressed in the context of virtually every generative topic you teach during the course. The unit-long understanding goals should be closely related to the overarching understanding goals.

Other Examples of Unit-Long Understanding Goals

Following are some examples of unit-long understanding goals. Note that each unit could have other understanding goals as well; for the sake of brevity, only one goal is listed here for each unit.

> *For a history unit with the generative topic "Freedom at a Cost: Understanding the Bill of Rights": "Students will under-*

stand the relationship between rights and responsibilities in a democratic society."

➤ *For a geometry unit with the generative topic "Finding Out What's True: Proofs in Mathematics":* "Students will develop their understanding of both inductive and deductive approaches to proving various statements (for example, that two triangles are congruent, that two lines are parallel, and so on)."

➤ *For a literature unit with the generative topic "Whodunits and How They're Done":* "Students will understand how authors create, develop, and sustain suspense in a plot."

➤ *For a biology unit with the generative topic "The Meaning of 'Life'":* "Students will understand how a biologist distinguishes between living and nonliving things."

Other Examples of Overarching Understanding Goals

Following are examples of overarching understanding goals:

➤ *For an American history course:* "How does our historical past make us who we are today?"

➤ *For a general science course:* "Students will understand that 'doing science' is not the process of finding facts but of constructing and testing theories."

➤ *For an algebra course:* "How can we use what we know to figure out what we don't know?"

➤ *For a literature course:* "Students will understand how metaphors shape the way we experience the world."

Goals That Do *Not* Emphasize Understanding

Many important goals of teaching and learning do not emphasize understanding. For example:

> ➤ Wanting students to know the multiplication tables. (Memorizing multiplication tables doesn't mean that students have an understanding of what they are or how and when to use them.)

> ➤ Wanting students to behave in class. (Appropriate behavior in class doesn't guarantee that students are focused on enhancing their understanding.)

> ➤ Wanting students to enjoy school. (Students often judge a discipline or domain in accordance with the way they are exposed to it. So it makes sense to look for accessible and exciting ways to teach subjects. However, there are plenty of topics and activities that students would consider fun that do not foster their understanding.)

While goals concerning student behavior or enjoyment may help create an atmosphere in which students' understanding can develop, it is important to distinguish these goals from understanding goals and to make sure that there is a balance between attending to understanding goals and to the other kinds of goals. It is also useful to note that knowing information, behaving well, and being engaged are not necessarily prerequisites for developing understanding. Often the very process of involving students in working toward important understanding goals leads to personal engagement, order in the classroom, and greater information retention.

Planning Unit-Long Understanding Goals

To begin planning your unit-long understanding goals, make a first pass at articulating those goals. Brainstorming is often a good way to do this. Ask yourself, "What understandings do I want my students to develop as a result of their work on this unit?" or "Why am I teaching this topic?" Write down whatever comes to mind. Many teachers find that working with a group is often helpful here.

Try stating your understanding goals as both questions and statements. Going back and forth between the two forms seems to help teachers refine their intentions.

Remember, you do not have to start with understanding goals. For many teachers it is easier to begin with generative topics or performances of understanding and then try to identify understanding goals.

No matter where you start, once you have drafted a unit, check to make sure your unit-long understanding goals relate to

> ➤ *Your overarching understanding goals.* Ask yourself, "What do I want my students to get out of their year's worth of work with me?"

> ➤ *The generative topic.* Ask yourself, "What is most important for my students to understand about this topic?"

> ➤ *The performances of understanding you have planned.* Ask yourself, "What do I want students to get from doing this activity?"

> ➤ *Your ongoing assessments.* Ask yourself, "What criteria will help me and my students figure out what they understand?"

If the answers to any of these questions don't match up closely to the understanding goals you've listed, revise either the understanding goals or the other parts of the framework until the "fit" is better.

> "Writing out the generative topic and the understanding goals forced me to focus on the big picture. I then could help students focus on their big picture for learning rather than little pieces of unconnected learning."
>
> **Nina Faraci, Special Education Teacher, Tewksbury, Mass.**

> "The link between understanding goals and understanding performances was important to me in my planning. I thought of lots of neat activities, but I had to cut some because they didn't serve my goals. I had many ideas for entry points, and I wanted to provide multiple opportunities for a variety of students to build and demonstrate their understandings, so making sure that understanding goals and understanding performances were closely connected helped me to trim my units."
>
> **Joyce Conkling, Seventh- and Eighth-Grade English Student Teacher, Arlington, Mass.**

Less is more: try to winnow your list to a handful of central understandings. If you are coming up with five or more understanding goals for a unit, consider the possibility that the material might be better presented as two or more units.

Planning Overarching Understanding Goals

In developing your overarching understanding goals, ask yourself, "When my students leave my class at the end of the course, what are the most important things I want them to take away with them?" Answering this question can be difficult. Often the goals that we consider most important are so deeply embedded in our thinking and teaching that we have a hard time articulating them. So if it seems that you have developed a list of overarching understanding goals that doesn't quite capture what you think is most essential, try some of the steps below.

➤ Review several units you have planned (either using this framework or in other ways). What common themes emerge? What understandings, skills, or concepts resurface time and again as you plan and teach?

➤ Ask your students what they hear you focusing on. Ask them what they think you want them to get from the class. And ask them what *they* want to get out of the class.

➢ As with unit-long understanding goals, try stating overarching understanding goals as both statements and questions.

Plan to revisit and revise your list of overarching understanding goals at least a couple of times during the year (perhaps once at the beginning of the second semester and once after you turn in final grades for the year).

Remember, your list of overarching goals is only a draft. To some extent this is true of all aspects of your planning and teaching: there is always room for improvement next year. But it is *particularly* true of overarching understanding goals. Of all the components of this framework, they are the hardest to articulate and take the longest to refine. Some teachers have found that it takes several years of periodically reworking their lists of overarching understanding goals in order to develop a version that they feel captures the essence of their course-long work with students.

> "Last year I felt I wasn't explicit enough with my students. I was really trying to be explicit, but I knew that I wasn't. I hadn't found exactly what things I wanted to be explicit about. And I felt that if I was explicit with my students while I was still unclear on my goals, I would just confuse them. So I didn't post throughlines last year. But thinking about them really helped me to zero in on the target, so that this year I could articulate the throughlines. And they still evolve. I just added another one and have revised some others."
>
> **Lois Hetland, Seventh-Grade Humanities Teacher, Cambridge, Mass.**

Teaching with Understanding Goals

Tell your students about them! State your unit understanding goals explicitly for your students at the start of each unit. State your overarching understanding goals (when you have drafted them) and talk about how the two lists relate to each other. Post your understanding goals (both unit and overarching) prominently in your classroom.

Allow your unit and overarching understanding goals to evolve during each unit and throughout the course. As you think of better ways to express the goals, alter their

> "When [my teacher] first handed out the list [of understanding goals], I just put it in my notebook and it really didn't sink in. But when I go back now and read it, it helps me understand, and I think, 'Why didn't I do this earlier?' . . . Now I know why she did the things she did. Now that we have that sheet, everything makes much more sense to me."
>
> **Maria, Ninth-Grade Student, Cambridge, Mass.**

wording. If other important goals emerge from your students, add them to the list.

Let your students know (or ask them to identify) the unit and overarching understanding goals they are working on as they carry out each performance of understanding. Refer to the goals often as you guide students through their performances. Making these connections will help your students understand the purposes that underlie their daily work.

Ask your students to write responses to the question form of your understanding goals periodically throughout the course or unit. This kind of understanding performance allows both you and your students to track their understanding as it develops from assignment to assignment.

☞ See Chapter Seven for more details about the connection between understanding goals and criteria for assessing student work.

Use your understanding goals as a starting point for developing assessment criteria. The things you most want students to understand should be the things you pay attention to in evaluating their work.

Common Questions About Understanding Goals

Aren't understanding goals a lot like behavioral objectives?

The statement form of understanding goals ("Students will understand . . .") may remind you of the phrasing of behavioral objectives ("Students will be able to . . ."), but there are important differences between the two. Behavioral objectives state what students will do; understanding goals, by

☞ See Chapter Six for further discussion of performances of understanding.

contrast, tell what students should learn from what they are doing. Understanding goals tell *why* the learning activities are important. Behavioral objectives, with their focus on action, are more closely related to understanding performances (though they are still different from them in crucial ways).

Doesn't spelling out understanding goals limit students' opportunities to explore? I want my students to develop understandings that are im-

portant to them, *not just understandings about what I think is important.*

If your approach to teaching is to individualize the curriculum for your students, or if you usually allow your students a large degree of autonomy in choosing and carrying out their work, then identifying understanding goals might seem limiting at first. However, you probably use an individualized approach to teaching because you feel that students learn some important things from it, and understanding goals can be adapted to make those things explicit for your students. Ask yourself what you want your students to learn from an individualized curriculum: perhaps how to generate questions based on their own interests and passions, or perhaps how to carry out projects in the way professionals in the discipline or domain do. These are important understanding goals. By making such goals explicit for students, you give them the opportunity to monitor their own growth and the power to separate the relevant from the irrelevant, the useful work from the interesting-but-distracting work.

> "I need to teach students what there is to understand and how to go about beginning to understand it. This much I knew before I used the Teaching for Understanding approach. What I did not realize was how much more efficient and productive the process of teaching inquiry would be if I made my goals explicit and asked the students to do the same. Far from limiting the richness, which is what I feared, the process enhanced it by developing clearer thinking in all of us. Teaching for understanding was not made easy, but it was made easier."
>
> **Lois Hetland, Seventh-Grade Humanities Teacher, Cambridge, Mass.**

REFLECTION

As you think about understanding goals, you might make some notes in your journal about the understanding goals you have for your students:

> "We always do really fun things at this school, but I wasn't always sure why. This year I always knew why, because I could look up at the throughlines when I couldn't figure it out."
>
> **John, Seventh-Grade Student, Cambridge, Mass.**

> ➤ *Think about a particular unit—perhaps one that you will teach soon. Ask yourself what you want your students to get out of the unit, and write down whatever comes to mind.*

➤ *To help refine your list, ask yourself which goals are really goals for student understanding and not goals about what information or behaviors you want students to master. Also ask yourself which goals capture essential aspects of the generative topic (if you already have one in mind) or the discipline you are teaching. Finally, ask yourself which goals you feel are most important. (You might try ranking them numerically.) For more about each of these points, review the "Key Features" section of this chapter.*

➤ *Try sharing your list of understanding goals with colleagues, who can provide feedback about the clarity of your goals. If you rank-ordered your goals, you might try justifying to the group why you chose the particular order you did.*

If you find yourself having difficulty in listing understanding goals, try working with one of the other parts of the framework. When you have written down your performances of understanding, criteria for ongoing assessment, or generative topic, come back to understanding goals and try again.

If you feel ready to begin to generate overarching understanding goals or throughlines, the following steps might be helpful:

1. *Review units you have already planned. Pick out goals that sound similar and that appear in two or three (or more) of those units.*

2. *Brainstorm other possibilities and add them to the list.*

3. *Set the list aside. Return to it periodically over the next few weeks to revise and add potential new overarching understanding goals.*

4. *Share your list with colleagues and ask for their feedback. From their experience working with you, do they think the list captures the most important aspects of your teaching?*

5. *Post a draft of the list in your classroom. Ask your students to help you see if these are the most important ideas as the year progresses. Ask them if it captures what they feel to be the most important things for them to learn.*

6. *Ask your students to write about the overarching goals at least three times: when you first post them, at midyear, and at the end of the year. Their responses will give you a lot of information about which overarching goals are helpful and which ones need work or are misdirected.*

7. *Return to the list at the end of the year. What goals might you add? Which might you delete or revise?*

Performances of
Understanding

6

with Dorothy Gould

Imagine trying to learn how to drive a car from a book or from lectures given by expert drivers. You study diagrams showing the position of the accelerator, brake, and clutch pedals. You read about the process of releasing the clutch as the accelerator is depressed. You memorize the appropriate braking distances ("allow twenty extra feet for each mile per hour in excess of fifty-five miles per hour"). An experienced driver explains how to gauge opportunities for merging into a stream of speeding traffic: "Look at the oncoming cars; estimate how fast they're going; think about how fast your car can accelerate; and when it looks safe, merge." You also hear lectures on how to parallel park. When you have read or heard about all of the various skills and techniques used in driving, you get behind the wheel for the first time and take your driving test.

Very few of us would pass the test under such circumstances. Certainly the books and lectures would have given us some information essential to driving a car, such as that it is necessary to signal before turning or that state law requires stopping for pedestrians in crosswalks. We might have memorized a great deal about the placement of the foot pedals and the "standard H" pattern of the stick shift. But we would not know how to use that knowledge judiciously in the infinite variety of circumstances that present themselves on the road at any given time. Without actual practice driving a car under a variety of conditions, with ongoing coaching and feedback from a driving instructor, we cannot learn to drive well and safely.

Students learning in school settings need the same kinds of experiences. They might acquire pieces of knowledge from books and lectures, but without the opportunity to apply that knowledge in a variety of situations with guidance from a knowledgeable coach, they will not develop understanding. Performances of understanding, or understanding performances, are the activities that give students those opportunities. Performances of understanding require students to go beyond the information given to create something new by reshaping, expanding, extrapolating from, applying, and building on what they already know. The best performances of understanding help students both develop *and* demonstrate their understanding. In the following case, consider how Denise, a ninth-grade science teacher, structures her students' work around performances of understanding:

Case Study: Developing Performances of Understanding for a Science Unit

In her teaching for understanding discussion group, Denise puzzled aloud over her ninth-grade science class: "They're smart kids. They could memorize this classification stuff in minutes and give it back to me on a test. But I'm really not sure it means anything to them except a grade." She recounted a dispiriting incident from the previous year in which the student who had scored the highest on the taxonomic description test was unable to make a good guess about the classification of an unidentified specimen when they examined it in class a few weeks later.

Having listened to the experiences of other teachers in the group who had used the Teaching for Understanding Framework, Denise knew that in order to help her students achieve more substantive learning, she would have to spend more time on the topic. This prospect posed a dilemma. The science department had worked hard to develop a standardized curriculum, and the chemistry teacher the students would have the following year would expect them to have covered certain material.

> Performances of understanding are more complex than simple memorization tasks and so require more time. Deciding which issues and concepts deserve more time and which need to be left out in order to create that time is a critical part of the planning process.

Denise felt a keen sense of responsibility to her department, her students, and their concerned parents. "They need to learn these things," she told the group. "But I'm barely getting through the syllabus now. If I spend too long on one topic, there are two or three others that they'll never learn about."

> For ideas about how to identify generative topics, see Chapter Four.

"But they're not really learning the stuff now," pointed out one group member, "they're learning it for the tests and then forgetting it." Denise agreed reluctantly. After some consideration she decided to omit a few topics from the last couple of weeks in the year in order to spend more time on classification. Denise believed that the concept of taxonomic classification was one of the central tools that biologists use to think about and examine the natural world. She would be willing to forego a few other topics in order to concentrate on it.

Having set aside eight days to teach scientific classification instead of the typical three, she began generating ideas about what her students might do during that time to develop their understanding of the topic. She thought of things like making up classification schemes, using these schemes

> The performances of understanding used in a unit need to closely match the unit's understanding goals. Denise's planning process—beginning with the performances and working backward to the goals—is one used by many experienced teachers, who often have a "gut sense," based on years of classroom experience, about what activities will be most fruitful for their students. Understanding goals emerge as one reflects on the value of the performances one feels are important for students to engage in. Then, once the goals are spelled out, the performances are adjusted to make sure they address the goals as directly as possible.

to categorize unfamiliar life forms and then defending these categorizations, looking at the etymology of the labels used in classifying, and so on.

After brainstorming these ideas for possible performances of understanding, she asked herself what she hoped students would gain by carrying them out. This process led her to articulate the following understanding goals:

Understanding goals are described in more detail in Chapter Five.

➤ Help students understand the importance of classification schemes.

➤ Help students understand the differences between and rationale behind folk and scientific methods of naming living things.

➤ Help students understand the bases for and uses of scientific classification.

Denise launches into a performance of understanding on the first day of the unit. In teaching for understanding, understanding performances are ubiquitous. They happen throughout a unit, from the beginning to the end, helping students both to develop and to demonstrate their understanding.

First Performance: Categorizing the Junk Drawer

Denise began the unit by emptying the contents of her home "junk drawer" onto a table at the front of the classroom. She then invited her students to describe what they saw. After writing their descriptions of the individual objects on the board, Denise asked her students to work in small groups to propose categories into which the objects could be put and to explain why they chose those particular categories.

Students offered many different kinds of classifications—by function, by composition, by position on the table, by estimated value—and explained their reasoning. Then they talked about why people might want to create categories for objects: How might such categories be useful? Had they ever found the need for creating categories and organizing things? After some discussion, students noted their responses in their journals. Denise then shared with them the understanding goals for the unit and explained that what they had just done was the first in a series of activities that would help them achieve these goals.

Second Performance: Categorizing Living Things

Denise began to nudge her students closer to a consideration of the scientific approach to classification. She next presented them with live specimens. She asked groups of students to work together to categorize the specimens using any criteria they thought appropriate. The groups then described their groupings to the class and explained why they chose them.

Denise then described the scientific classification system and explained briefly the characteristics of each category. She reminded the class of the second goal for the unit: to understand the differences between folk and scientific classifications. She asked them to compare their classification schemes with the scientific method and to comment on the differences they saw. What kind of information did each kind of classification scheme provide? When might each scheme be appropriate? When might each not be appropriate?

Third Performance: Applying the Taxonomic Classification

Denise then provided the class with another group of specimens and had each group of students choose an organism to examine. The students observed the specimens for two class periods, noted and described their characteristics, and then attempted to determine their species. They named a kingdom, phylum, order, family, and genus for each specimen, giving both

> The two categorization exercises described here have many of the characteristics of typical introductory performances of understanding. They are called *introductory* performances of understanding in the Teaching for Understanding Framework because they invite students to begin "messing about" with the issues before a lot of information is given. These kinds of performances allow teachers to see what students already understand about a topic. They also help illuminate some of the many possible ways the topic might relate to students' interests, observations, and questions.

> Here Denise provides direct information to her students in a ten-minute minilecture. Centering classroom practice on performances of understanding does not mean that one never gives students information. It does mean that such information is given as the need arises in the context of performances of understanding. Similarly, specific skills students need to develop can also be identified and addressed in the context of performances of understanding.

In many classrooms, as students work on performances of understanding, the teacher often becomes a "floating coach," moving from small group to small group or student to student, responding to questions, and redirecting small-group work. Occasionally the teacher will bring the class together for a minilecture to provide further information that students need or to address a problem that has surfaced in many groups' or individuals' efforts.

the Latin and common names. At each level of identification the students had to explain the key characteristics that suggested placement in the particular category they chose. During this time, as she did during most small-group work, Denise "floated" around the room, listening to conversations, asking questions to help push students' thinking about which characteristics to attend to, and encouraging students to think about what they had learned in the previous discussions that would be useful to them in this task. After the two class periods the groups came together to discuss questions and confusions that had arisen during the activity.

Fourth Performance: Exploring a Particular Problem in Classification

The third, fourth, and fifth performances are examples of "guided inquiry" performances of understanding. They are typical middle-of-the-unit performances that focus students on particular problems and issues related to the generative topic and the understanding goals.

In watching her students work, Denise noticed their tendency to rely heavily on behavior as a criterion for classification. To help them think more critically about this issue, she designed another activity. She had the students gather in their small groups to consider these questions: How is behavior useful in classifying living things? When is behavior misleading or inaccurate? They identified some examples of how using behavior would help in making a taxonomic classification. They also came up with some counterexamples, times when behavior might be misleading or inaccurate. The small-group work was followed by a whole-class discussion, after which Denise encouraged the small groups to rethink and revise their initial opinions.

Fifth Performance: Debating Alternative Methods

Next Denise brought in an article from *Science News* that recounted some of the key issues in the ongoing debate among sci-

The Teaching for Understanding Guide

entists over the "standard" approach to classifying living organisms. She asked her students to generate other reasons why scientists might prefer one method of classification over another. The students then divided into two groups and debated which method they would prefer. After fifteen minutes she asked each side to choose a new position and then continue the debate.

Asking students to explain their reasoning by giving evidence to support their conclusions (either orally or in writing) is a typical component of a performance of understanding. Understanding performances should give students the opportunity to make their thinking explicit.

In the reflections the students wrote afterward, they discussed which arguments they found most convincing and why.

Final Performance: Individual Projects

To wrap up the unit Denise had her students carry out two projects on an individual basis. For the first project the students examined six organisms in the lab and identified the kingdom to which they belonged. The instructions for the performance encouraged them to make educated guesses about the phyla of the organisms as well, and to explain their choices. Next they had

These final projects are typical end-of-unit, or "culminating," performances of understanding. Such performances are more complex than preceding ones and require students to draw together a number of different understandings developed in previous performances.

to create their own dichotomous key that could be used to classify the organisms by an individual who had not studied taxonomy. (As part of the assessment process, Denise invited several taxonomy-naive teachers and students into the class to try to use the dichotomous keys to classify the organisms.)

For the second project the students received the following instructions: "Pretend that you are an animal conservationist looking for a rare species of animal that has been sighted only once by zoologists. Zoologists tell you that the animal was spotted in the northern Brazilian rain forest and that it is a mammal. What clues does this give you about the possible appearance and nature of the animal? Repeat the same exercise with a plant described only as 'resembling a dayflower.' Compare the amount of information provided by the scientific name *Compositae* and the common name *dayflower*. Which is more useful for this endeavor? Why?" For this project students submitted a draft of their work to a classmate for peer review before handing in a final draft to Denise. Both the peer reviewer and the student worked with a criteria sheet that Denise had handed out with the instruction sheet.

For a final performance of understanding, Denise translated each of the three understanding goals into a question:

➤ What is the importance of classification schemes?

➤ What are the differences between and rationale behind folk and scientific methods of naming living things?

➤ What is scientific classification based on? What kind of information does it provide? In what situations might it be useful?

She then asked the students to write as much as they could about each of the questions in order to help her (and themselves) gauge their understanding.

Key Features of Performances of Understanding

"The projects were very helpful. If we [hadn't done] the projects, I wouldn't have got it. [My teacher] would have just gone over it in class, and I would have said, 'Okay.' But when we reviewed for the final I would have forgotten all about it and would have had to go over it again. . . . But I think because we did the project, and we had to go over and over it every single day, and we had to know it to be able to do the project, I learned it. The projects helped because we had to use the ideas, the notes, the text, and the assigned homework."

Shannon, Tenth-Grade Student, Braintree, Mass.

Performances of understanding are activities that require students to use what they know in new ways or situations to build their understanding of unit topics. In performances of understanding students reshape, expand on, extrapolate from, and apply what they already know. Such performances challenge students' misconceptions, stereotypes, and tendencies toward rigid thinking.

Performances of understanding help students build *and* demonstrate their understanding. Although a "performance" might sound like a final event, performances of understanding are principally learning activities. They give both you and

The Teaching for Understanding Guide

your students a chance to see their understanding develop in new and challenging situations over time.

Performances of understanding require students to show their understanding in an observable way. They make students' thinking visible. It is not enough for students to reshape, expand, extrapolate from, and apply their knowledge in the privacy of their own thoughts. While it is conceivable that a student could understand without performing, such an understanding would be untried, possibly fragile, and virtually impossible to assess. It is a little like the difference between a daydream about how you would like to behave in a particular situation versus how you actually behave when the situation arises: the daydream and reality might turn out to be similar, but then again they might not. So performances of understanding involve students in publicly demonstrating their understanding.

"In my other math classes, we never did projects, and I had trouble understanding. Then when we started doing projects [in this class], everything seemed to click, and then I got most of the stuff. When we started out we had to use angles and shapes and rays. I had to think of how to do a poster with them. For my poster I wanted to do something totally different from everyone else, so I drew a city. And as I was drawing, I realized that I do use these things all the time! Most of the shapes are the same, and it's not as hard as people think."

Brian, Tenth-Grade Student, Braintree, Mass.

Other Examples of Performances of Understanding

Following are some examples of performances of understanding for units in different academic areas. Since performances of understanding are always connected to one or more specific understanding goals, the applicable unit-long understanding goal or goals (in statement form only) are provided with each example.

"[I knew I understood] because when we did different examples. . . . I could really explain them. . . . I could explain different things that I didn't know before, so I believe that I understand."

Demetra, Eleventh-Grade Student, Belmont, Mass.

➤ *For an English unit with the understanding goal "Students will understand how to detect the clues (both obvious and subtle) that authors give about what their characters are like":* Students pick one event described by Charlotte in *The True Confessions of Charlotte Doyle*. First they write down all the things they can tell about Charlotte from the way she describes the event. Then they compare their answers with those of their classmates, noting and discussing the differences in interpretation. Second, students pick two other characters involved in that event and make up an entry for each of those characters' diaries. The object is for students to weave into each entry clues that will help readers understand who these characters are.

➤ *For a social studies unit with the understanding goal "Students will understand that history is always told from a particular perspective and that understanding a historical text means understanding who wrote it":* Students compare two accounts of the beginning of the Revolutionary War—one that claims the British fired the first shot and one that claims the colonists did. They then discuss why the two reports might be different and how they could find out what really happened. They use some of these strategies to figure out which (if either) of these accounts is the more plausible and then present their explanation to the class.

➤ *For a mathematics unit with the understanding goals "Students will understand how percentages can be used to describe real-world happenings" and "Students will understand how to represent numerical information in clear graphs":* In small groups, students collect and compile data about school attendance over the course of two weeks. They calculate the percentage of students who fit various categories (percentage of students absent, percentage present, percentage tardy, and so on). They then create graphs to represent their data visually, collect feedback from the class, and revise their graphs accordingly.

➤ *For a science unit with the understanding goal "Students will understand how light and images are affected as they pass through 'everyday lenses' like magnifying glasses, telephoto camera lenses, and so on":* Students experiment with a collection of concave and convex lenses and a flashlight. They try to find combinations of lenses that act like a magnifying glass, a telephoto lens, and a wide-angle lens. They then draw diagrams to illustrate how light travels through these combinations of lenses.

Performances That Do *Not* Necessarily Show Understanding

Just as there are many important goals that are not understanding goals, so are there many important performances that neither build nor demonstrate students' understanding. For example:

➤ Writing memorized definitions on a vocabulary test.

➤ Answering questions (either on a test or in discussion) about facts reported in a textbook.

➤ Writing from memory the formula for solving quadratic equations.

➤ Following the directions in a textbook for conducting a science experiment.

➤ Taking true-false or short-answer tests.

Although these performances are not performances of understanding, they could serve other important functions in fostering student learning.

> "When I'm planning, I tend to start with performances of understanding. I'll find something that kids are really going to enjoy and that they'll get a lot out of. Once I pick that, then the question is, 'How can I help them to tie in to the disciplinary context, to understanding something about themselves, and all those understanding goals?' I ask myself, 'What are these activities demonstrating to me, and how are they helping the students?'"
>
> **Lois Hetland, Seventh-Grade Humanities Teacher, Cambridge, Mass.**

Planning Performances of Understanding

You might begin planning by brainstorming ideas for possible performances of understanding. You could start by thinking about activities your students have done in the past that seemed especially productive.

If you have already identified your understanding goals, look at the list of possibilities for performances of understanding that you have generated and identify the ones that best seem to support those goals.

If you have not identified your understanding goals yet, look at the list of possibilities and ask, "Why do I want students to do this?" This will help you to articulate your understanding goals. Once the goals have been identified, you can examine the performances again and perhaps revise them so that they more closely foster the understandings you consider most important.

For the performances you select, think about how to build in opportunities for students to get feedback on and revise their work as they carry out those performances.

When you have generated a number of performances of understanding, try to sequence the performances so that they occur throughout the unit, from the beginning to the end. Think about the following kinds of performances as you work:

> *Introductory performances.* These are the performances of understanding that usually come first in a unit. They give your students a chance to explore the generative topic a bit. They also give you an opportunity to gauge students' current understanding of the topic. The possibilities for connections between students' personal interests and the topic emerge from these explorations.

> *Guided inquiry performances.* In these kinds of performances of understanding, students focus on developing their understanding of particular problems or aspects of the generative topic that you feel are especially important. Guided inquiry performances typically occur in the middle of units.

> *Culminating performances.* These more complex, concluding performances of understanding give students

The Teaching for Understanding Guide

a chance to synthesize and demonstrate the understandings they developed during the other performances of understanding.

Does your final contingent of performances of understanding for a unit include a variety of performances that give students a chance to develop and demonstrate their understandings in a number of different ways? If many of the performances are similar (for instance, if many performances require students to "explain in their own words" or to adopt and debate one side of a controversy), try revising some of them to allow for greater diversity in how students develop their understanding.

Teaching with Performances of Understanding

As students are engaging in performances of understanding, help them to make connections between the performances and the understanding goals that the performances should help them achieve. Try thinking of yourself as a "floating coach"—keep a general eye on the progress of your students and listen for common questions, sources of confusion, and issues that should be addressed in whole-group discussion or lectures.

In talking with students, ask often for them to explain their answers. Ask them to give reasons for their answers, to offer supporting evidence, and to make predictions in the course of whole-group discussions or written reflections about the performances of understanding.

"In designing performances of understanding, I really have to think hard about where the kids are. When I designed the lever project [in which students had to figure out where to place the fulcrum in order to balance two different weights], I wanted them to have something challenging to do. At the same time, I didn't want there to be a thousand variables where they could really get lost. The way I solved it was to structure it: I predrilled holes [where the fulcrum could be placed] in the meter stick so that there would only be nice even proportions for them to work with. I controlled the number of variables and the number of different setups they could have. So I decided to lead them in a direction that would allow the biggest chance of [their] making sense of the patterns they were seeing. . . . Now, did I make things too easy for them? This is something I struggle with all the time. How can the performances be clear enough so that they lead students to the right place, but not so narrowed down that the students don't see the bigger picture? It's something I have to consider all the time."

Eric Buchovecky, Eleventh-Grade Physics Teacher, Belmont, Mass.

Finally, provide students with the criteria by which the performances will be assessed, and give them opportunities (especially in more complex performances) to assess their own and others' work and then to revise their work before handing in a final product.

Common Questions About Performances of Understanding

Although performances of understanding sound interesting, what about basic skills? My students still need to learn to write complete sentences.

Basic skills are important, and in classrooms that really focus on understanding, a lot of time is spent providing students with the practice and support they need to develop these skills. However, without understanding why those skills are important or when they are useful, students are not likely to learn them well or to use them in appropriate situations. Incorporating basic skills practice into the context of performances of understanding allows students to see why such skills are important.

My students already do a lot of hands-on activities in the classroom. Are these the same as performances of understanding?

Perhaps they are. What is essential about performances of understanding is that they are closely tied to important understanding goals. For instance, having students play a game of *Jeopardy* in order to learn history facts might be considered a "hands-on" activity, but it is not a performance of understanding.

What about typical activities like class discussions and writing papers—are these performances of understanding?

They can be. If the paper is more than a mere report, if the student puts forth an opinion or point of view and defends it with evidence and arguments, she is certainly engaging in a performance of understanding. If the discussion requires that students puzzle out new problems or questions, draw conclusions, make predictions based on evidence, debate issues, and so on, then the discussion becomes a performance of understanding for those students who are participating.

Do students really need to do something in order to understand? Sometimes I can tell by the lights in their eyes that they understand.

It *is* important for students to perform their understanding. That "light" might be due to the fact that they have just remembered that today is Friday and this is their final class before the weekend! You may gather important clues about what students understand by interpreting their faces and gestures. Especially in the early stages of a unit, such quick, informal assessments are useful for gauging when to shift the focus or draw a conversation to a close. However, the only way to know with certainty how well students understand is to ask them to carry out some task that requires them to go beyond what you have told them or what they have read in a textbook.

"Kids aren't asked to do long-term projects very often in school, so they don't know how to face them. They need to start off with something that has lots of products and lots of natural milestones embedded in it, so that they feel like they're accomplishing something along the way. I'm always telling students, 'Don't worry about that whole paper now. Just worry about the part that's due on Wednesday.' I make sure that what we do in class really gives them something to draw on as they do their longer-term work, so they won't feel like they're starting from nothing. In the class on myths, students have to produce a ten-page paper that deals with all these archetypes as they arise in modern literature. I start them reading the book [that they'll do their paper on] at the beginning of the semester. But rather than have them read it and then analyze it and write a review, I ask them leading questions as they read, like, 'Does the story have a hero? Why do you think so?' I'm leading to the archetypes they're going to see in later stories. When they read the myths, they'll start to recognize these archetypes. And then when they have to write the final paper, they'll have these notes to draw from."

Joan Soble, High School English Teacher, Cambridge, Mass.

What's the difference between performances of understanding and understanding goals?

Understanding goals tell what students should understand. Performances of understanding are what students do to develop and demonstrate those understandings.

REFLECTION

In reflecting on the performances of understanding you use in your own practice, it can be helpful to think about both those activities that you feel have helped your students deepen their understanding and those with which you are not satisfied. You might make a list in your journal of each kind of performance.

Using the Key Features section in this chapter, review the lists you have made to identify the strengths of the successful performances and to think about how to revise the unsuccessful ones. You might think in particular about whether or not there are clear goals for each performance and whether students might be able to "get through" a performance without understanding (a sure sign that the performance needs to be revised!). You might think, too, about whether or not your performances can be sequenced into introductory, guided inquiry, and culminating performances.

If you have already worked through the Reflection section in Chapter Five, you could use the goals you developed there as a starting point: what performances would support each of the understanding goals you identified? With colleagues, you might want to brainstorm other performances that could support each goal and then refine the list using the Key Features section in this chapter.

(If you have not yet worked through Chapter Seven, you might save the notes you have made here and refer to them when you reach the Reflection section in that chapter.)

Ongoing Assessment

7

with C. Eric Bondy and Bill Kendall

How can we assess accurately and fairly what our students have learned? This is a question every teacher wrestles with. But when understanding is the purpose of instruction, the process of assessment is more than just one of evaluation: it is a substantive contribution to learning. Assessment that *fosters* understanding rather than simply evaluating it has to be more than an end-of-the-unit test. It needs to inform students and teachers both about what students currently understand *and* about how to proceed with subsequent teaching and learning.

This kind of assessment occurs frequently in many situations outside of school. Imagine a basketball coach working with his team during a practice session. He might begin by asking the team to concentrate on a few particular skills or plays. As the players scrimmage he studies their moves, measuring them against his standards of skillful basketball playing. He usually pays particular attention to the strategies and skills he asked the players to concentrate on at the start of practice. He analyzes the problems when the team falls short and, as the team plays, tells them how they can improve their performance. Occasionally he stops the practice session, brings the team together to provide more sustained feedback, and gives the players new tasks based on his assessment of their performance.

This kind of coaching continues through actual games as well. Games conclude not only with a score that tells the team how well it performed but also with debriefing sessions in the locker room in which the coach and the team hash out what went well and what they need to work on before the next game.

Or think of a director's work as she prepares a troupe of actors for a stage production. Each rehearsal is a continuous cycle of performance and feedback as the actors work through the scenes in the play. The director gives initial instructions, offers advice and further direction while each scene is in progress, and convenes more formal feedback sessions at various points during the rehearsal.

This integration of performance and feedback is exactly what students need as they work to develop their understanding of a particular topic or concept. In the Teaching for Understanding Framework this is called "ongoing assessment." Ongoing assessment is the process of providing students with clear responses to their performances of understanding in a way that will help them improve the next performance.

The following case study describes how one teacher built opportunities for ongoing assessment into a geometry unit.

> The process of ongoing assessment not only provides students with feedback about their work but also allows both teacher and students to assess how well students' understanding is developing.

Case Study: Embedding Ongoing Assessment in a Geometry Unit

Lisa had already had some experience working with the framework when she began to design a unit on area for her tenth-grade geometry class. During the previous semester, she had experimented with hands-on performances, such as using art and drawing to help students understand parallel lines and transversals. The activities had effectively engaged her students, but she had not been sure about how much they understood as a result of their engagement. To remedy this situation she decided to give more attention to the assessment process in planning and carrying out the new unit.

In collaboration with a friend who taught geometry at a neighboring school, Lisa reviewed her work from the previous semester and considered how to help her students develop an understanding of the topic of area in the new semester. As she looked back over her students' work she realized that two things had impaired her ability to assess their understanding and provide them with useful feedback.

First, the performances she had asked her students to carry out were ones she had not assigned before. Consequently she did not have a clear image of what they should look like. In examining her students' work once it was completed, she could begin to see who had a grasp of the important points and who did not. However, she had never articulated clear performance criteria for her students, either before or while they worked. In the absence of such criteria, the grades she had assigned had felt a little arbitrary, both to her and to her students.

> Criteria that are clearly articulated and closely related to unit understanding goals make up the first of two important characteristics of ongoing assessment in the Teaching for Understanding Framework. In cases like Lisa's, where a performance is new to the teacher as well as the students, an initial set of criteria can be spelled out when the assignment is given and then publicly revised if necessary as students' work on the performance progresses.

The second problem had to do with the way she had designed her performances of understanding and feedback opportunities. For each understanding goal there had been only one supporting performance of understanding. Also, Lisa had not given her students a chance to revise that one performance once they had carried it out. Consequently there was no way for her students to use the feedback she provided and no way for her to judge whether their understanding had developed over time. The assessment process helped to evaluate but not deepen her students' understanding.

> The second important characteristic of the ongoing assessment process is the presence of frequent opportunities to provide feedback that helps students improve their performances of understanding.

Even though Lisa's initial focus is ongoing assessment, she quickly finds herself thinking about performances of understanding. This shift is a common feature of the planning process. Because the different parts of the framework are so intimately linked, beginning with one part of the framework often leads quickly to considering other parts of it.

Because the criteria for evaluating performances of understanding should mirror the unit-long understanding goals, articulating those goals is essential to developing a useful ongoing assessment process.

For more detail on developing understanding goals (both unit-long and overarching), see Chapter Five.

Lisa realized she was going to need a clearer and more defined approach to assessing her students' work if the performances she assigned in her geometry class were really going to support learning. Since at least part of the problem was rooted in the design of the performances, she began her planning by thinking carefully about how to develop and sequence performances of understanding that would build on one another and give her students the chance to achieve one or two understanding goals.

Lisa decided to develop a project that could be broken down into several stages. Such a project would allow her students to receive feedback about their work at various points and would let her monitor more closely their developing understandings and provide support when they needed it.

To begin designing such a project, she considered both her generative topic and her understanding goals for the unit. Her generative topic for the unit was "Designing Places." Her unit-long understanding goals were as follows:

1. Help students understand how to use what they know about area to find out what they don't know about it—specifically, help them understand how to use familiar formulas for computing area to figure out formulas they don't know. (How can we use what we know to find out what we don't know?)

2. Help students understand how formulas for calculating area are derived and applied. (Where do formulas for area come from? How are they useful?)

3. Help students understand their own best approach to solving "messy" (as opposed to "textbook") problems. (What are my best strategies for solving difficult problems?)

With these goals in mind, Lisa devised the following project for students to work on over the course of several weeks:

Our city has been given a substantial amount of money by a lottery winner to build a community center. The donor, a mathematician who also loves dancing, has certain requirements that must be met if her money is to be used to build the center. She has asked that the first floor be designed so that people can have a place to go to dance and socialize. The dance floors are to be constructed in the shape of different polygons. Her specifications are as follows.

The total area of the first floor must be between 6,500 and 9,500 square feet. There should be five rooms and hallways arranged as needed to make access to the rooms, the front door, and the fire doors relatively easy. Each room must contain a dance floor. You may choose the size and location, but there must be at least one dance floor in each of the following shapes: rectangle, triangle, circle, hexagon, and parallelogram (which may not be a rectangle). Each dance floor must be approximately half of the total area of the room. Further, in each room there must be a section in the shape of a trapezoid for the DJ or band to set up (the area of this section can be included in the total area of each room).

Lisa decided to break down the students' work on this project into five steps—four introductory and guided inquiry performances of understanding that would build toward the fifth, culminating performance of understanding. For each of the performances she articulated criteria for assessing the students' work and created opportunities for students to receive and incorporate feedback from her as well as from classmates and self-assessments.

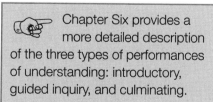
Chapter Six provides a more detailed description of the three types of performances of understanding: introductory, guided inquiry, and culminating.

First Performance: Planning to Solve the Problem

The students created a plan for solving the problem. This plan included stating the problem in their own words, listing the steps they would take to solve it, identifying the things they already knew that would help them, identifying the things they would need to know, and finally, sketching out an approximation of the floor plan (without actually figuring the areas).

> To articulate her assessment criteria, Lisa refers back to her understanding goals. What she wants her students to understand should be the primary criteria she uses to grade their performances.

Since her goal for this step of the instruction was to help her students develop their understanding of how to draw on what they already know and how to begin to address "messy" problems (the first and third unit-long understanding goals), Lisa decided to focus primarily on two criteria in assessing this portion of her students' work. First, she wanted to see how well they could identify what they already knew about solving the problem by considering the work they had already done in the class. Second, she wanted to see how many details they attended to in formulating and asking questions about the project. Since this was an introductory performance that the students would be

> Feedback can be provided informally, particularly in the early stages of work as students get started and the teacher learns how well students understand (or don't understand) particular aspects of the topic.

carrying out as a whole class, she decided to keep the process of assessing and giving feedback fairly informal: she would tell the class about the assessment criteria, but she would let them assess themselves. She would offer them her own assessment verbally in the context of the discussion.

Second Performance: Understanding How to Find Area

The students discussed the various areas they needed to know how to compute in order to solve the problem. Working from a formula they already knew (the one used to compute the area of a rectangle), they used a hands-on activity to derive other formulas. They drew the required shapes (parallelograms, triangles, and so on) on graph paper, cut them apart, and reshaped them into a rectangle. Then they used the formula for a rectangle to calculate the overall area and to figure out a formula for calculating the area of each shape.

Since this was another introductory performance, designed primarily to help Lisa learn what her students knew and how well they could use it, she continued to assess informally. She asked the students to rate

> In providing feedback from a variety of perspectives, Lisa does not have everyone evaluate everything all the time. Sometimes students assess themselves; sometimes Lisa evaluates them; sometimes they provide feedback for one another.

themselves on how well they were able to use the formula they knew to discover new ones. She also asked them to write down their questions as they worked so she could address them during class discussion time. The discussion offered Lisa the opportunity to provide general feedback based on her observations of the class's work.

Third Performance: Beginning to Solve the Problem

The students then worked in small groups to design one room of the community center. The design included a sketch of the floor plan with dimensions and area marked. The students also wrote a description of how they carried out their work and explained the decisions they made.

For this performance Lisa devised more formal assessment criteria and feedback sheets. Once the small groups had completed their efforts, she asked them to make

> The feedback from each stage of the project helps students go on to the next phase.

short presentations to the class on their work. The rest of the class used the assessment criteria and the feedback sheets to let the presenting group know how well they had done and to suggest how they might want to improve their current floor plan as well as the floor plans they had yet to do. Lisa also asked the students to write individual reflections about their own group's work: Which parts of the problem had been particularly difficult or easy to address? Which problem-solving strategies had proved fruitful? Which had not? The groups used their reflections on the process as well as the feedback from Lisa and their classmates to carry out the next performance. (The reflection exercise also supported the third unit-long understanding goal.)

> By measuring her students' performances against the established criteria (which are closely related to the understanding goals), Lisa is able to gauge what other kinds of support her students need in order to carry out the next phase of the work in a way that will help them further develop their understanding.

During the course of these presentations and reflections, two problems became apparent to Lisa. First, some of the students were still confusing the computation of area with the computation of perimeter. Second, many groups seemed to be struggling with the process of solving problems cooperatively. To address these issues Lisa used the following two days to provide more direct instruction on each problem to the whole class. Then, armed with feedback from peer assessments and self-assessments, the students moved on to the fourth performance.

Fourth Performance: Designing the Entire Floor Plan

The students, working in the same small groups, completed the entire floor plan of the community center (including a revised version of the floor plan they had drafted for the third performance). These floor plans were presented to the entire class. To aid their oral presentations, the groups created diagrams with the areas labeled. They prepared statements that showed how they had met all of the parameters of the project and explained some of the key decisions they had made in doing so.

Again, Lisa and the students used a checklist of assessment criteria. Like the one they had used for the third performance, this one included items such as "Meets all parameters stipulated in the original assignment," "Offers a logical explanation for each choice made," and so on. Before the final presentations, the groups paired up and offered one another feedback on draft presentations. When they made their final presentations to the class, they collected feedback and suggestions about both the strengths and the problems in their work. They used this feedback to prepare for the final performance.

Before the final performance, Lisa discussed with the class the assessment criteria they had been using. She asked them to think about the projects they had seen and to decide whether there were criteria they wanted to add or revise. Several students had questions that were cleared up by simplifying the language on the feedback sheet. Others suggested some modifications based on their analysis of the good and the not-so-good projects they had seen (for example, including labels of the rooms, doors, and so on, along with the dimensions of each wall, made the floor plan easier to read). The modified feedback sheet, with points assigned to each item, became the students' guide for the final project.

> Here Lisa invites her students to help revise the criteria by which their final performances of understanding will be assessed. Students can also be involved in earlier stages of assessment criteria development, particularly if they have models (both good and bad) of the final performance or product that they can observe as they generate criteria.

Fifth Performance: Preparing Individual Papers

Each student made her own personal modifications to the plan her group had developed and wrote a description of her final floor plan. Students used feedback received during the oral presentation to revise and refine their efforts. In addition, Lisa asked each student to write a reflection that assessed the strengths and weaknesses of his or her project and described what the student had learned about each of the three unit-long understanding goals.

> Note that over the course of the five-part unit, accountability has moved from informal to formal and from being group-oriented to being focused on the individual. This shift often happens as students progress from collaborative and informal introductory performances to more formal projects carried out by individuals at the end of a unit.

Before handing in their final projects, the students filled out a feedback sheet, rating themselves on how well they had achieved each of the standards and explaining their scores. Lisa evaluated the revised floor plans, the written descriptions of the work, and students' reflections on their understanding of the unit goals.

Key Features of Ongoing Assessment

There are two principle components of the ongoing assessment process: establishing assessment criteria and providing feedback.

The criteria for assessing each performance of understanding need to be

> "With authentic questions, we may not know enough about the answers to set the assessment criteria in advance. However, you can set them with students as you go along."
>
> **Lois Hetland, Seventh-Grade Humanities Teacher, Cambridge, Mass.**

➤ Clearly and explicitly articulated at the beginning of each performance of understanding (though they may well evolve over the course of the performance, especially if it is new to the teacher as well as the students).

➤ Relevant (closely related to the understanding goals for the unit).

➤ Public (everyone in the classroom knows and understands them).

Feedback needs to

➤ Occur frequently, from the beginning of the unit until its conclusion, in conjunction with performances of understanding. Some feedback may be formal and planned (such as feedback on a presentation); some may be more casual and informal (such as responding to a student's comment in a class discussion).

➤ Provide students with information not only about how well they have carried out past performances but also about how they might improve future ones.

➤ Inform your planning of subsequent classes and activities.

➤ Come from a variety of perspectives: from students' reflections on their own work, from classmates' reflecting on one another's work, and from the teacher.

Other Examples of Ongoing Assessment

Following are further examples of ongoing assessment. Because ongoing assessment occurs in the context of performances of understanding, which in turn are anchored to understanding goals, each of the examples below includes unit-long understanding goals (in statement form only) and performances of understanding as well as a description of criteria and feedback for ongoing assessment.

➤ *For a unit in a writing class with the understanding goal "Students will understand the process of writing an effective persuasive essay":*

Performance of understanding: Students write an essay in which they pick a controversial issue and argue for their personal stance on that issue.

Criteria for ongoing assessment: Teacher and students codevelop the criteria for the essay. To do this the teacher presents students with two brief sample essays written about the same issue. The first argues the thesis effectively; the other is noticeably less well executed. By comparing the two, the students (with guidance from the teacher) generate criteria for identifying a good, persuasive essay (a clear position statement, concrete examples to support the position, consideration and refutation of counterarguments, and so on). The teacher makes a copy of the list of criteria for each student in the class so the students can use it in the feedback process.

Feedback for ongoing assessment: Using the criteria they have defined with the teacher, the students complete a first draft of their essay and write a short reflection assessing it. They share this draft with a classmate, who also provides a short written piece that reflects on how well the essay meets the criteria. Equipped with these two reflections, the students revise their essays and submit final drafts to the teacher. Both the teacher and the students assess the final essays by rating on a scale of one to ten how well the students satisfied each of the criteria, with a brief written explanation of the rating.

➤ *For a mathematics unit with the understanding goals "Students will understand percentages and their real-life uses in describing*

> "Self-assessment has helped me figure out how I'm doing compared to what [my teacher] thinks I'm doing. She makes a point of slowing us down, and we take home our folder to select our best five pieces of what we consider well done, and [this] helps us to gain focus. It is important to know what you know compared to what the teacher thinks."
>
> **Lisa, Seventh-Grade Student, Cambridge, Mass.**

> "[Explicit criteria] helped. It is good to know where you want to go. It's not good to be walking around in the dark."
>
> **Brian, Tenth-Grade Student, Braintree, Mass.**

data" and "Students will understand surveying as a tool for collecting data that can be expressed mathematically":

Performance of understanding: Students develop surveys to collect information from fellow students about their health (say, the number of colds each person catches in a year) and some variable that the students think will be related to healthiness (percentage of after-school time spent exercising, for example). They decide how to use graphs and charts to represent their data most effectively. (For example, 80 percent of students who report getting sick less than once a year spend 50 percent or more of their after-school time engaged in some exercise.)

Criteria for ongoing assessment: The teacher shares with the students a sheet that describes the two categories of assessment criteria for their work: qualities of an effective survey and characteristics of an effective use of percentages in survey work.

"The criteria [checklist] sort of opened my mind to what I needed to improve. . . . It's like having a calculator: you might know the answer, but you just check to be sure. . . . And how is that helpful? It's just like an insurance for me when I am doing my work."

Tom, Eleventh-Grade Student, Cambridge, Mass.

Feedback for ongoing assessment: The students share drafts of their surveys with one another for feedback and critiquing. They submit a first draft of their graphs and charts to the teacher for comments. The final draft is submitted with a self-evaluation that the teacher includes as part of the final grade.

➤ *For a social studies unit with the understanding goal "Students will understand various forms of government and their advantages and disadvantages":*

Performance of understanding: Small groups of students are randomly assigned a form of government (monarchy, oligarchy, democracy, and so on) and given a brief description of how laws are made under that type of government. Within the groups, each student is assigned a role (monarch, president, or dictator; wealthy owner of a factory; laborer living near the poverty line, and so on) by drawing a slip of paper from an envelope. The groups then have to decide how to levy taxes in their "country," making their decision according to the form of government they have been assigned. After the groups are given some time to work through the problem, the students form new small groups, with each group including at least one member from each of the original groups. In these groups they share their experiences and discuss the advantages and disadvantages of each particular approach to governance. Each student then writes a paper describing her initial group experience with the assigned government and comparing it to the other groups' governments.

Criteria for ongoing assessment: Each student's final paper is assessed based on how accurately the student's initial group carried out their particular government type's decision-making processes and the sophistication of the comparisons the student makes between that form of government and the others. These criteria are shared with the class before they begin writing.

Feedback for ongoing assessment: The teacher has the students exchange first drafts of their papers with other members of their initial groups so that they can check one another's accuracy in describing the first groups' work. She then has them share a second draft with her so that she can check their understanding of various forms of government. In cases where one or more of the small groups seem not to have captured the essential aspects of the assigned government, she provides the students with feedback about where to find more information about that government so that they can revise their work.

Assessment That Does *Not* Support Understanding

Some assessment practices do not support students' understanding. For example:

➤ Evaluating student performances without having made the assessment criteria explicit beforehand.

➤ Evaluating student performances only at the end of a unit—even if the evaluation is based on a performance of understanding (and not, say, on an end-of-unit short-answer test). Assessment helps build understanding only if students can use it to refine and support future efforts. Although it is true that we usually have to give students a final grade and move on to the next unit, the process that leads up to that final grade should include a number of cycles of performance and feedback.

Planning Ongoing Assessment

It is usually easiest to think about specific ongoing assessment procedures in the context of performances of understanding or activities you have planned.

Your understanding goals are a useful tool for generating the criteria by which to assess your students' performances. For instance, if your aim in asking your students to write a paper is to build their understanding of a particular concept, then the paper needs to be assessed primarily on the basis of how well they demonstrate understanding of that concept, not on whether they have used complete sentences and appropriate paragraphing.

It is also important to build in opportunities at the beginning of and throughout a unit for assessing students' developing understanding. If assessment happens only at the end of a unit, it is not "ongoing," and it cannot help your students develop and refine their understanding. To make sure students have plenty of opportunity to learn from their work, you might try to create opportunities within performances of understanding for your students to give feedback to one another or to get feedback from you as they work.

Try to balance formal and informal feedback across the performances in a unit. Also, try to provide a variety of perspectives in each unit by using self-assessment, peer assessment, and teacher assessment of student work.

Finally, build in time to help your students develop the skills they will need to provide one another and themselves with useful feedback. Self-reflection and peer assessment does not come easily to most students, but both can be learned.

Teaching with Ongoing Assessment

Even if you have a sense of what the criteria for a particular performance should be, try inviting students to develop the assessment criteria themselves by looking at models or mock-ups of similar performances.

Once the criteria have been established, post them prominently in the classroom. Through formal and informal discussions, help students to see how the criteria relate to the understanding goals.

Model for your students how to provide feedback that both tells them how well they are doing and gives them information about how they might do

> "My students are not the kind I can turn loose and say 'Do a reflection.' I get very, very short pieces of writing from them. When we first start writing short stories, what works for me is to say, 'Here are someone else's eight criteria for what makes a good short story. For each criterion, write a short reflection about how well the short story that you've written meets it.' When there's that much structure, then they do great. Eventually they get to the point where they can start to generate that structure themselves."
>
> **Joan Soble, High School English Teacher, Cambridge, Mass.**

> "I put ongoing assessment in the middle of the process of planning and teaching for understanding. For me it's not just assessing the students; it's also assessing myself and the curriculum and my teaching. I'm always asking, 'How well are my students understanding?' But I'm also asking, 'How well are the performances helping them to understand? Are these good understanding goals? Are they appropriate for these kids? How could they be better?'"
>
> **Bill Kendall, Ninth- and Tenth-Grade Algebra and Geometry Teacher, Braintree, Mass.**

better. Portfolios and reflection journals can be useful tools for students to track their learning over time.

Finally, try using assessment opportunities not only to gauge how well your students are doing but also to examine and re-shape your curricula and practice.

Common Questions About Ongoing Assessment

This kind of assessment sounds very time-consuming. How do teachers manage it?

Looking carefully at student work *does* take time, but the simple fact of the matter is that if we don't look closely at that work, we have no idea what students are really understanding and what they are missing. And without feedback, students have little chance of figuring out what they need to work on.

> "I found that when I really focused students on just a few things, if I told them that I was only going to grade them on, say, two or three aspects of their work, then they really made strides on those two or three things. Too many criteria just overwhelms them."
>
> **Bill Kendall, Ninth- and Tenth-Grade Algebra and Geometry Teacher, Braintree, Mass.**

It helps to keep in mind the fact that most of us are already assessing our students all the time. Every time they ask a question or respond to one of ours, we think about what those questions and responses reveal about their learning. The trick is to figure out how to let our students benefit from that continual weighing process and how to help them understand the criteria for assessment as well as we do. Several techniques can help make this process more manageable:

1. Not every performance needs to be assessed formally. Feedback can be given verbally and informally as students work in small groups or as the teacher leads a class discussion.

2. Keep assessment criteria boiled down to just those few items that you really care about (the ones stated in the understanding goals). This not only makes the grading and feed-

back process easier for you but also en-
sures that students will spend their time
and energy well.

3. Take time to teach your students how
to talk with one another about assessment. If everyone understands the criteria for a performance and has had
practice providing supportive critiques,
then students can coach and provide
feedback for one another, even though
you are the one who ultimately gives
the grade.

*What's the difference between performances of
understanding and ongoing assessment?*

Understanding performances are the
things students do to develop and demonstrate their understanding. Ongoing assessment is the process by which students get feedback about what they do, based on clearly
articulated criteria for successful performances. It is, in
essence, the process of reflecting on performances in order to
gauge progress toward the understanding goals.

> "Kids will give constructive
> feedback to each other if
> they think they are helping someone
> to get a better grade. We have peer
> feedback before kids turn in work.
> Then they get to revise. It's part of
> sharing the burden of assessing, if
> kids can give meaningful feedback.
> But you have to be careful. I had
> kids assess a final project and it was
> a joke: they all gave each other A's.
> But if you circulate drafts ahead of
> time and say, 'You know what I'm
> looking for, and I'm the one who's
> going to grade these, so you help
> each other,' then they give more
> constructive feedback."
>
> **Joan Soble, High School English Teacher,
> Cambridge, Mass.**

REFLECTION

*Designing the ongoing assessment process for a unit can be a particu-
larly challenging step in the planning process. One way to begin might
be to take stock of your current approach to assessment. Think of a unit
you have carried out recently. What formal and informal opportunities
were there for your students to receive feedback? How clear were the
criteria for assessing their performances? (You could ask your students
to describe their impressions of the criteria used for a recent assignment*

or to explain why they think they received a particular grade on an assignment.)

If you are keeping a reflection journal or working with a group of colleagues, try making notes about or discussing the ways in which your approach to assessment is similar (or dissimilar) to the approach described in this chapter. (The lists in the Key Features section of this chapter may be particularly helpful.) With which aspects of your approach to assessment are you satisfied? Which aspects of it would you like to work on?

If you are starting your planning process with ongoing assessment and find that you are having difficulty, you might try working on developing understanding goals or performances of understanding first and then return to ongoing assessment later.

If you have already read the Reflection section in Chapter Six, try generating ideas for assessment criteria and feedback for the performances of understanding that you listed there. You can use the list under Key Features and discussions with your colleagues to help you refine the ongoing assessment process you develop.

Tips and Tools for Planning and Teaching

Planning curricula and classes is a very personal activity. Each of us approaches the process differently, depending on our preferred working style, the available time and resources, the subject matter, and the specific group of students for whom we are planning. Clearly no one way of planning will suit every teacher or every set of circumstances. However, as teachers have used this framework over time, a few key ideas about the planning and teaching process have emerged—strategies, techniques, and pointers that many have found helpful in getting started. These suggestions are collected in this chapter.

Getting Started

Choose a "chunk" of curriculum that feels right to you. Some people prefer to start small—perhaps by focusing on a short, two- to three-day unit. Others decide to work on larger units, often in the two-week to two-month range. Still others prefer not to think about the duration of a unit at all in the beginning; rather, they generate ideas for units first and then decide how much time to spend on them. There is no "correct" length for a unit of instruction when using the Teaching for Understanding Framework.

The important thing is to work with a slice of curriculum that feels comfortable to you.

For people who prefer to tackle the big picture first, another approach is to begin not with a single unit but with the design of a semester- or year-long class. Teachers using this strategy typically map out the throughlines and generative topics for the semester or year and then move on to planning individual units. (Most people who are just beginning to use this framework find it much easier to begin by developing a single unit rather than a whole course. For this reason the tips and tools in this chapter focus primarily on unit development.)

Decide whether to start from scratch or to revise an established unit. The framework has proven useful not only for generating new units but also for rethinking familiar ones. When beginning with an existing unit, most teachers find it helpful to choose one about which they have genuine questions or concerns—perhaps a unit that did not work well last year or one in which some activities seemed successful but others were problematic.

Begin where you want to begin. Which aspects of your practice would you like to focus on? Which pieces of the framework seem the most interesting to you? Which do you think might be the most helpful in your work? The answer to any of these questions can help you find a good starting place. Although this book has presented the components of the framework in a particular order, starting with generative topics and ending with ongoing assessment, you can begin your planning with any of them. Many teachers prefer to begin with performances of understanding, envisioning worthwhile activities for their students to do and then asking, "Why are these activities important? What do I want

> "This kind of planning focuses my energies so that I can work 'smarter,' not necessarily harder. It keeps me prepared so that I'm ready for student questions without . . . throwing me off base. By planning ahead and knowing my throughlines, I can encourage student questions and find a place for them."
>
> **Rozanne Gette, Fourth-Grade Teacher, Snoqualmie, Wash.**

> "We had trouble initially trying to word our understanding goals. So we planned backwards. We developed a list of things we wanted students to do and then thought about the goals—why we wanted them to do it."
>
> **Eileen Gardner, Sixth-Grade Teacher, Tewksbury, Mass.**

my students to get out of them?" These questions then lead them to articulate understanding goals for the unit. For others it is easier to begin by thinking about the various concepts and issues that might serve as generative topics and then to move on to identifying goals and performances.

If working with one piece of the framework proves difficult, move on to another part and come back to the first part later. If you have trouble articulating a set of understanding goals you feel comfortable with, for example, try developing performances of understanding and come back to the goals later. If coming up with a generative topic turns out to be a stumbling block, try thinking about understanding goals or performances of understanding instead; ideas for a generative topic might emerge from those thoughts. Ultimately all the pieces of the unit will need to be closely related (the understanding goals will need to be supported by appropriate performances of understanding, the criteria for assessing those performances will need to be closely related to the understanding goals, and so on). But in the initial planning stages it often helps to allow yourself the flexibility of moving from piece to piece.

Remember that in unit and course planning, less is more. In every domain, at every grade level, there are many, many generative topics, understanding goals, and performances of understanding that can help students build understanding. No teacher has time to incorporate all of them into her teaching, and it's just as well! By delving deeply into a few well-chosen topics, working toward a few important goals, and engaging in a few complex performances, students will develop more useful and lasting understandings than they will if they have to work on many things at once—*even very generative, important things.* Choices always have to be made, and difficult as they may be, we owe it to our students and ourselves to make them.

"Defining the understanding goals has really shifted the focus of our planning from 'teach it all' to 'what do we really need to teach?' Having team planning time has helped us to make important connections across the disciplines as well. When students know that several classes have common goals, they really transfer their learning. They comment on what they've learned in other classes and how it connects with our current study."

Paula Wynn, Eighth-Grade Language Arts Teacher, Norfolk, Va.

A Planning Process

Here is one way of planning with the framework that some people have found helpful:

1. Brainstorm around each part of the framework.

2. Refine the brainstormed lists, using reflection questions.

3. Finalize (more or less) the unit or course plan.

Various suggestions and planning sheets in this chapter can help to explain and support each step.

1. Brainstorming

Why This Step Is Useful

Because planning time is scarce, it may be tempting to focus on the first idea that comes to mind. Resisting that temptation and trying instead to generate a range of possibilites for topics, goals, performances, and assessment processes can yield more productive results. No matter which part of the framework you begin with, ideas about the other parts will surface as you work. Thinking about understanding goals will spark ideas about assessment, which in turn will trigger new ideas about performances of understanding, which might lead you to consider other understanding goals, and so on. Beginning with a brainstorming session about all parts of the framework (rather than definitively stating your generative topic, then moving on to understanding goals, and so on) can help you to capture all of these loosely associated but potentially powerful ideas as they emerge.

If you decide to begin with a brainstorming session that involves all parts of the framework, do not be too concerned about getting your thoughts into the right categories of the framework. If you can't tell whether an idea belongs in the "generative topic" section or the "understanding goals"

> "Sometimes I'm tempted to go with the first idea that comes to mind—especially if it seems like it is one that will interest my students. It's useful for me to have this kind of planning structure that really makes me ask questions about my initial good ideas: Why do I think it's good? Will my students really gain understanding if they do these activities? How will I know?"
>
> **Melissa Collins, High School French Teacher, Beverly, Mass.**

The Teaching for Understanding Guide

section, simply list it in both places and move on. The refining step will give you the opportunity to sort things out.

What Helps When Brainstorming

First, it is extremely useful to have a place to write down your ideas as they come to you. Some people find it helpful to use a large piece of chart paper and a marker. Others prefer to work on notebook paper. Whichever you use, setting up a chart like the one in Figure 8.1 has the advantage of allowing you to see and brainstorm about all parts of the framework simultaneously. (If you decide to start by concentrating on developing a single unit rather than a course, you might want to ignore temporarily the box for overarching understanding goals, or throughlines.)

Second, talking with colleagues and students is helpful. The point of brainstorming is to generate a lot of ideas quickly. Working with others helps this process dramatically. If you are planning a longer unit, you might even want to carry out several brainstorming sessions—one by yourself, one with colleagues, and one with your students (What would they like to learn about? What kinds of performances might they be interested in trying?).

2. Refining

Why This Step Is Useful

The framework is a powerful tool for helping to focus the teaching and learning processes on those concepts, skills, and ideas that are most important for students to learn. To create this focus effectively, each piece of the curriculum (the topic, goals, performances, and assessment) needs to be closely related to and supportive of the other pieces:

➢ Understanding goals need to focus students' attention on the most important aspects of the generative topic.

➢ Performances of understanding need to engage students in developing exactly those understandings articulated in the understanding goals.

<table>
<tr><td colspan="2" align="center">OVERARCHING UNDERSTANDING GOALS, OR THROUGHLINES
"The things I most want my students to understand after this course or year are . . ."
Statements such as "Students will understand . . ."</td></tr>
<tr>
<td align="center">GENERATIVE TOPIC</td>
<td> UNIT-LONG UNDERSTANDING GOALS "Students will understand . . ." and
"The questions I'd like my students to be able to answer are . . ."</td>
</tr>
<tr>
<td> PERFORMANCES OF UNDERSTANDING "Students will build toward achieving the understanding goals by . . ."</td>
<td> ONGOING ASSESSMENT "Students will get feedback on their performances by . . ."
(That is, how will they know how well they are doing?)
"The criteria for each performance will be . . ."</td>
</tr>
</table>

FIGURE 8.1   *Brainstorming Chart*

The Teaching for Understanding Guide

➤ Criteria for ongoing assessment need to be closely related to the understanding goals. Feedback needs to help students improve their performances of understanding.

➤ Unit-long understanding goals need to support the overarching understanding goals for the course.

Refining the brainstormed list, then, is the process of selecting and revising generative topics, goals, performances, and approaches to assessment so that they are closely related to one another and help focus students' work on developing a few central understandings.

What Helps When Refining

First, it helps to use a set of reflection questions like those in Figure 8.2. Once you have brainstormed a list of possibilities (or once you have a draft of a unit), the questions listed in the figure can help you identify and refine the "best bets" for each of the framework's elements. These questions reflect the criteria for each element of the framework, but the most important criterion to keep in mind is that *each element needs to support and be supported by the others.*

Second, just as for brainstorming, it helps to talk with colleagues and students. Often when planning—especially when planning very familiar material—it is easy to assume rather than to spell out the connections between topics and goals or between goals and performances. Responding to the questions of people who are not as intimate with the material or who have a different perspective (because they teach a different grade level or subject matter or have taught the same thing in a different way) can both generate new ideas and sharpen developing ones.

3. Finalizing (More or Less)

Why This Step Is Useful

Creating and writing down a final plan helps with several things. First, it makes clear and explicit the essential features of the lesson, unit, or course. Second, documented efforts can be revisited

Overarching Understanding Goals, or Throughlines:

❑ Capture what you believe to be the *most* important things for students to learn in your class?

❑ Phrased as questions *and* as statements (such as "Students will understand . . ." or "Students will appreciate . . .")?

❑ Relate closely to generative topics and understanding goals for the units you want to create or have created?

Generative Topic:

❑ Central to one or more disciplines or domains?

❑ Interesting and exciting to students?

❑ Interesting and exciting to you?

❑ Provides opportunities for students to make connections to other classes as well as life outside of school?

❑ Has related resources and materials to make topic accessible to students?

Unit-Long Understanding Goals:

❑ Closely related to throughlines?

❑ Focus on central aspects of generative topic?

❑ Capture what you think is *most* important for students to understand about the generative topic?

❑ Take the form of a question *and* a statement?

Performances of Understanding:

❑ Require students to demonstrate the understandings stated in your understanding goals?

❑ Call for students to apply learning in new situations?

❑ Allow students to build *and* demonstrate understanding?

❑ Challenge students' misconceptions, stereotypes, and tendencies toward rigid thinking?

❑ Sequenced so that students can engage in them throughout the unit, from beginning to end?

❑ Allow students to demonstrate their understanding in a variety of ways (written work, artistic endeavors, and so on)?

Ongoing Assessment:

❑ Includes clear, public criteria?

❑ Uses criteria closely related to understanding goals?

❑ Provides frequent opportunities for feedback throughout the unit's performances?

❑ Provides feedback that tells students how well they are doing and how to do better?

❑ Offers opportunities for multiple perspectives?
  ➤ Teacher assessing student
  ➤ Students assessing one another
  ➤ Students assessing themselves

❑ Provides mix of formal and informal feedback?

FIGURE 8.2   *Criteria for Refining the Brainstormed List*

and revised more easily in the future. Finally, the written plan becomes a useful tool for talking with students, colleagues, parents, and administrators about what is happening in your classroom and why.

However, as the Teaching for Understanding Framework suggests, understanding develops through carrying out challenging activities: actually completing a unit with a group of students (certainly a challenging performance of understanding for teachers!) often improves teachers' understanding of the unit and how to teach it better. You may find yourself flooded with new and possibly better ideas as you teach. While some of the new ideas gained will need to be saved for future units, some can be incorporated even as the lesson progresses: adding or rewording goals to state more clearly the important desired understandings; working with students to refine the criteria for assessing particular performances of understanding, and so on. Making such changes while the unit is in progress is fine as long as the changes are public and explicit.

> "This approach to teaching for understanding has helped me to focus on what the real task of teaching and learning is about. Having to make the understanding goals explicit has taught me the importance of clarity, both for me as a teacher as well as for my students. It has reinforced in me the idea that having hidden agendas only creates confusion and discourages motivation."
>
> **Sr. Patricia Leon Agusti, School Director, Bogotá, Columbia**

What Helps When Finalizing (More or Less)

First, it is helpful to lay out the whole unit in one place. To do this you might try using the Teaching for Understanding Graphic Organizer (see Figure 8.3). Laying out a final draft of a unit in this way facilitates making visual connections between

➤ Unit-long understanding goals and overarching understanding goals (or throughlines).

➤ Unit-long understanding goals and the performances that support them (by writing in the numbers of the relevant goals in the box next to the performances).

➤ Performances of understanding and ongoing assessment processes.

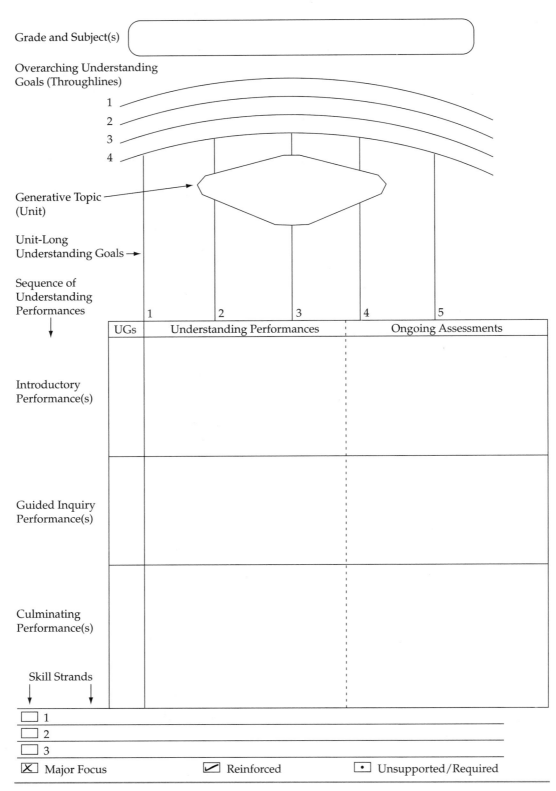

Grade and Subject(s)

Overarching Understanding
Goals (Throughlines)

1
2
3
4

Generative Topic
(Unit)

Unit-Long
Understanding Goals →

Sequence of
Understanding
Performances
↓

| | | UGs | Understanding Performances | Ongoing Assessments |

1   2   3   4   5

Introductory
Performance(s)

Guided Inquiry
Performance(s)

Culminating
Performance(s)

Skill Strands

☐ 1
☐ 2
☐ 3

☒ Major Focus   ☑ Reinforced   ⊡ Unsupported/Required

FIGURE 8.3   *The Teaching for Understanding Graphic Organizer*

© 1997 Lois Hetland and the President and Fellows of Harvard College (on behalf of Project Zero).

The Teaching for Understanding Guide

➤ Performances of understanding and the skills students
need to carry them out.

Second, it helps to keep in mind that even finalized plans will
change and develop once they are put into practice. Some teachers
find that labeling every lesson plan a "draft" helps them remember that there is always the potential for change and improvement.

Keep in mind that the graphic organizer in Figure 8.3 is only
one way to represent and document a teaching for understanding unit. Some teachers prefer a more narrative form in which
they simply write out the goals, performances, and assessments
in paragraphs. Some teachers prefer a weblike graph in which
the generative topic for the unit is at the center of the page, the
unit-level understanding goals appear in a circle around the
generative topic, and performances of understanding and ongoing assessment procedures are written in an outermost circle,
with arrows showing which performances are connected to
which goals. Because the space on a regular sheet of paper is limited, some teachers prefer to transfer this graphic organizer (or
another one of their own making) to larger paper or to write out
each element of the framework on a separate sheet.

It is also important to keep in mind that the space on this
graphic organizer is artificially limited to accommodate all the
pieces of the framework. For instance, there are only four slots
for overarching understanding goals and five slots for unit-long
understanding goals, and the spaces for introductory, guided inquiry, and culminating performances of understanding are all
the same size. This does not mean that the you must limit yourself to four overarching goals and five unit-long understanding
goals or that you must have equal numbers of introductory,
guided inquiry, and culminating performances in your units.
There is no correct number of goals or performances, and you
should feel free to modify the graphic organizer to suit the needs
of your unit plan. See Figures 8.4 and 8.5 for examples of how
the graphic organizer might be used.

Finally, the graphic organizer is designed to support the
planning of units, not year- or semester-long classes. If you are

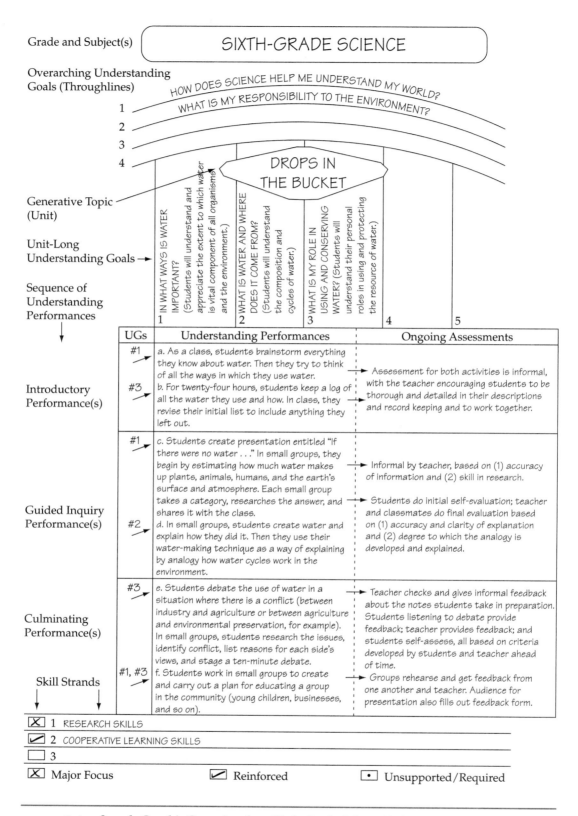

Grade and Subject(s)

SIXTH-GRADE SCIENCE

Overarching Understanding
Goals (Throughlines)

HOW DOES SCIENCE HELP ME UNDERSTAND MY WORLD?

WHAT IS MY RESPONSIBILITY TO THE ENVIRONMENT?

1

2

3

4

DROPS IN THE BUCKET

Generative Topic
(Unit)

Unit-Long
Understanding Goals →

Sequence of
Understanding
Performances
↓

1 IN WHAT WAYS IS WATER IMPORTANT? (Students will understand and appreciate the extent to which water is vital component of all organisms and the environment.)

2 WHAT IS WATER AND WHERE DOES IT COME FROM? (Students will understand the composition and cycles of water.)

3 WHAT IS MY ROLE IN USING AND CONSERVING WATER? (Students will understand their personal roles in using and protecting the resource of water.)

4

5

	UGs	Understanding Performances	Ongoing Assessments
Introductory Performance(s)	#1	a. As a class, students brainstorm everything they know about water. Then they try to think of all the ways in which they use water.	Assessment for both activities is informal, with the teacher encouraging students to be thorough and detailed in their descriptions and record keeping and to work together.
	#3	b. For twenty-four hours, students keep a log of all the water they use and how. In class, they revise their initial list to include anything they left out.	
Guided Inquiry Performance(s)	#1	c. Students create presentation entitled "If there were no water . . ." In small groups, they begin by estimating how much water makes up plants, animals, humans, and the earth's surface and atmosphere. Each small group takes a category, researches the answer, and shares it with the class.	Informal by teacher, based on (1) accuracy of information and (2) skill in research.
	#2	d. In small groups, students create water and explain how they did it. Then they use their water-making technique as a way of explaining by analogy how water cycles work in the environment.	Students do initial self-evaluation; teacher and classmates do final evaluation based on (1) accuracy and clarity of explanation and (2) degree to which the analogy is developed and explained.
Culminating Performance(s)	#3	e. Students debate the use of water in a situation where there is a conflict (between industry and agriculture or between agriculture and environmental preservation, for example). In small groups, students research the issues, identify conflict, list reasons for each side's views, and stage a ten-minute debate.	Teacher checks and gives informal feedback about the notes students take in preparation. Students listening to debate provide feedback; teacher provides feedback; and students self-assess, all based on criteria developed by students and teacher ahead of time.
Skill Strands ↓ ↓	#1, #3	f. Students work in small groups to create and carry out a plan for educating a group in the community (young children, businesses, and so on).	Groups rehearse and get feedback from one another and teacher. Audience for presentation also fills out feedback form.

[X] 1 RESEARCH SKILLS

[✓] 2 COOPERATIVE LEARNING SKILLS

[ ] 3

[X] Major Focus   [✓] Reinforced   [·] Unsupported/Required

FIGURE 8.4 *Sample Graphic Organizer for a Sixth-Grade Science Unit*

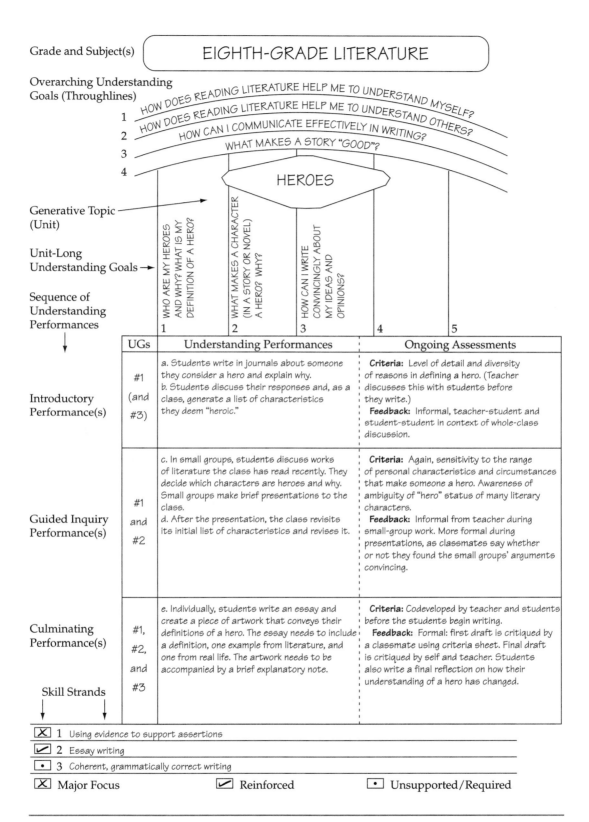

Grade and Subject(s)

EIGHTH-GRADE LITERATURE

Overarching Understanding
Goals (Throughlines)

1 HOW DOES READING LITERATURE HELP ME TO UNDERSTAND MYSELF?

2 HOW DOES READING LITERATURE HELP ME TO UNDERSTAND OTHERS?

3 HOW CAN I COMMUNICATE EFFECTIVELY IN WRITING?

4 WHAT MAKES A STORY "GOOD"?

HEROES

Generative Topic
(Unit)

Unit-Long
Understanding Goals

Sequence of
Understanding
Performances

1 WHO ARE MY HEROES AND WHY? WHAT IS MY DEFINITION OF A HERO?

2 WHAT MAKES A CHARACTER (IN A STORY OR NOVEL) A HERO? WHY?

3 HOW CAN I WRITE CONVINCINGLY ABOUT MY IDEAS AND OPINIONS?

4

5

	UGs	Understanding Performances	Ongoing Assessments
Introductory Performance(s)	#1 (and #3)	a. Students write in journals about someone they consider a hero and explain why. b. Students discuss their responses and, as a class, generate a list of characteristics they deem "heroic."	**Criteria:** Level of detail and diversity of reasons in defining a hero. (Teacher discusses this with students before they write.) **Feedback:** Informal, teacher-student and student-student in context of whole-class discussion.
Guided Inquiry Performance(s)	#1 and #2	c. In small groups, students discuss works of literature the class has read recently. They decide which characters are heroes and why. Small groups make brief presentations to the class. d. After the presentation, the class revisits its initial list of characteristics and revises it.	**Criteria:** Again, sensitivity to the range of personal characteristics and circumstances that make someone a hero. Awareness of ambiguity of "hero" status of many literary characters. **Feedback:** Informal from teacher during small-group work. More formal during presentations, as classmates say whether or not they found the small groups' arguments convincing.
Culminating Performance(s) Skill Strands	#1, #2, and #3	e. Individually, students write an essay and create a piece of artwork that conveys their definitions of a hero. The essay needs to include a definition, one example from literature, and one from real life. The artwork needs to be accompanied by a brief explanatory note.	**Criteria:** Codeveloped by teacher and students before the students begin writing. **Feedback:** Formal: first draft is critiqued by a classmate using criteria sheet. Final draft is critiqued by self and teacher. Students also write a final reflection on how their understanding of a hero has changed.

☒ 1 Using evidence to support assertions

☑ 2 Essay writing

⊡ 3 Coherent, grammatically correct writing

☒ Major Focus   ☑ Reinforced   ⊡ Unsupported/Required

FIGURE 8.5   *Sample Graphic Organizer for an Eighth-Grade Literature Unit*

planning a unit and have not yet identified your overarching understanding goals, simply leave those spaces blank and work with the rest of the page.

Teaching with the Framework

"I really need to think of the planning process as a long-term investment. The goals I set for my class this year were a moving target. The goals kept shuffling their importance in my mind. I'd think, '*This* is the central issue for my class,' and then I'd think, 'Wait a minute, that's not what I really need to do; I need to reshape that.' And so I'd keep changing the priorities. With this class I feel like I've given them several different visions. And I keep thinking, 'Boy, this is a horrible year.' But I think there's hope, in that when I sit down next year I'll have a much clearer idea about what goals I do want to set and which ones are realistic. I keep saying, 'This isn't working so well now, but it's leading me to a better understanding of how to go about it next year.'"

Eric Buchovecky, Eleventh-Grade Physics Teacher, Belmont, Mass.

Mentally prepare for challenges as well as successes. When our students engage in new, complex tasks, we do not expect perfect results. When students get discouraged by their failures and want to label a particular task or subject or class (or their teacher or themselves) "stupid" or unworthy of their time, we try to coax them into a more productive frame of mind. We help them to appreciate the progress (however small) that they *have* made, and we encourage them to learn from their mistakes or to tackle the same problem in a different way. Similarly, when we try out new lessons or units in our classes, the results may fall short of our hopes. Giving ourselves and our colleagues the same encouragement we would give to our students in the face of difficulties can mean the difference between lapsing into old practices and continuing to develop professionally through experimentation and revision.

Examine closely what students do and say. The evidence of the success of a unit lies in the degree to which students develop their understanding of the goals. Since student understanding is embedded in the performances they carry out during the unit, we need to slow ourselves down enough to look closely at these performances—both the processes and the finished products. Two practices can help support this examination:

➤ Acting as a coach in the classroom. If your students are engaged most of the time in performances of under-

The Teaching for Understanding Guide

standing, you will have some time to circulate through the room as they work, watching their efforts, asking questions, making suggestions, identifying who needs more help, and so on. This style of teaching gives you far more opportunity to learn about what your students are learning than the kind of teaching that keeps you continually talking to the whole class from the front of the classroom. (This is not to say that lecturing is always a bad thing or that you should never stay in the front of the room to lead students step-by-step through some activity. However, if either of those approaches is your predominant teaching style, then you will necessarily give up many opportunities to see what your students are actually learning.

➤ Looking at and discussing student work with students and colleagues. Taking time to really examine one or two pieces of student work in the company of colleagues or the students themselves provides a wealth of information about the students, the assignment, and the classroom. Several helpful structures exist for guiding such conversations: the "Tuning Protocol" developed by the Coalition of Essential Schools and the "Collaborative Assessment Conference" developed at Project Zero are two of many currently being used in schools. You might even talk with your colleagues about developing your own structure for guiding conversations about student work.

Frequently revisit the understanding goals with your students.
Both the unit-long understanding goals and the overarching understanding goals, or throughlines, are useful tools for checking students' developing understanding. If the question forms of the goals are posted prominently in your classroom, you can simply ask your students periodically to write out their responses to those questions. Comparing the responses students give

> For descriptions of The Tuning Protocol, The Collaborative Assessment Conference, and other processes for looking collaboratively at student work, see *Student Work/Teacher Learning*, edited by David Allen, Teachers College Press (New York) 1998.

early in the unit with those they give later (or, if you are working with throughlines, the responses they give in the beginning of the year or course with those they give at the end) is a quick way for both you and your students to assess their progress.

Give yourself time to reflect alone and, if possible, with colleagues. Time is precious, but reflection does not need to be lengthy to be useful. You might try simply using the checklist in Figure 8.6 as a quick mental review at the end of the day. The checklist can also serve as the basis for discussion with colleagues. You might also periodically review the understanding goals—perhaps at the beginning of the school day in the few minutes before students arrive: How will the day's activities help students to achieve those goals? How can you remind students of those goals?

Finally, pace yourself. Developing and carrying out performances of understanding—especially lengthy and complex ones—can be time- and energy-consuming. Many teachers who work with the framework like to intersperse teaching for understanding units with periods of time in which students work on other kinds of skills: memorizing multiplication tables or vocabulary words, doing more text-based kinds of problem solving, or hearing a few lectures on a particular topic. For teachers who face the omnipresent pressure of a standardized curriculum, such an approach can also provide a way to balance the demands of covering the material with those of supporting students' understanding. (Students, too, often appreciate a break between complex, time-intensive projects.)

> "I find I need to pace myself [in] planning these kinds of units. They are a lot of work—extremely rewarding for both me and the students, but still a lot of work. So sometimes we go in depth, and sometimes we spend a couple of weeks focusing on some pretty straightforward skills. And then we go back in depth on the next topic. Maintaining the balance is important."
>
> **Bill Kendall, Ninth- and Tenth-Grade Algebra and Geometry Teacher, Braintree, Mass.**

REFLECTION

Once you have had a chance to read through the planning and teaching ideas in this chapter, you might try thinking about, writing about, or talking with colleagues about some of the following questions.

YOU KNOW YOU ARE TEACHING FOR UNDERSTANDING WHEN . . .

The learning is generative:

❑ Instruction is focused around a few central topics.

❑ The topics are personally significant for you and your students.

❑ Students are actively engaged in their work.

❑ An atmosphere of genuine inquiry pervades the classroom.

The understanding goals are clear and explicit:

❑ Overarching goals or throughlines are explicitly stated and posted in the classroom.

❑ Goals for particular units are closely related to overarching goals.

❑ You and your students regularly discuss and reflect on unit-long and overarching goals to help students make the connection between what they are doing and why they are doing it.

Students are working on performances of understanding almost constantly:

❑ Students work actively in varied formats: pursuing projects and reflecting alone, collaborating and conferencing in small groups, and interacting in whole groups.

❑ Students are thinking and making that thinking visible in the contexts of performances of understanding that challenge their misconceptions, stereotypes, and rigid thinking.

❑ Students can explain why they are doing what they are doing.

❑ You spend your time coaching, conferencing, leading, participating in discussions, and sometimes lecturing.

❑ The room is filled with student work, both finished and in process.

❑ Responsibility and authority for the work is shared between you and your students.

The assessment is ongoing:

❑ Students engage in cycles of drafting, reflecting, critiquing, responding to, and revising their own and others' work.

❑ You and your students share responsibility for assessment.

❑ Everyone assesses work according to stated criteria and standards for quality, which are closely related to the understanding goals.

❑ Assessment is often casual, conversational, and spontaneous; periodically it is more formal, recorded, and planned.

❑ Self-reflection occurs frequently, in a variety of forms.

FIGURE 8.6 *Teaching for Understanding Reflection Checklist*
Developed by Lois Hetland

Tips and Tools for Planning and Teaching   **105**

How does this approach to planning compare to how you typically plan? How might you adapt some of the planning suggestions in this chapter to make them more useful to you?

Review the checklist in Figure 8.6 with colleagues. Does this list delineate characteristics that fit with your image of a classroom devoted to understanding? What other qualities or characteristics would you add to the list?

If you have time to plan units in consultation with colleagues, you might try the following steps in a series of collaborative planning meetings.

1. *Ask everyone to come to the meeting with an idea for a unit they would like to plan.*

2. *Divide up the time for the first meeting so that everyone's idea for a unit is given an equal amount of time as the focus of a group brainstorming session. Assign a timekeeper to the group, and devote a few minutes (perhaps five or ten minutes for a group of four) to brainstorming about each unit (you can sketch out the chart in Figure 8.1 on paper large enough for the whole group to see).*

3. *Everyone can come to the second meeting with a rough sketch of the unit, drawing on the brainstormed ideas. (It is fine at this point to have a really sketchy unit outline.)*

4. *Give each person some time to share his or her unit. (If the group is large, you might try breaking into smaller groups of three or four and asking group members to bring enough copies of their unit drafts to share with everyone.) Once the unit has*

been described briefly, invite the group to use the questions on the "Criteria for Refining the Brainstorm List" (Figure 8.2) to review the unit and make suggestions about ways to improve it.

5. *Repeat the drafting-sharing-revising process as often as group members need to or have time for.*

6. *You might find it helpful to continue talking with your colleagues once the unit is under way. Colleagues can serve as a "support group" to celebrate your successes and to help generate ideas for overcoming difficulties.*

Teaching for Understanding and Other Educational Practices

9

It seems as though every year a new approach (or two or three or four) to teaching and learning takes center stage in the education arena, only to be nudged out of the limelight a short time later by a newer technique or curriculum. On the one hand this proliferation of materials and approaches is encouraging and helpful. It gives us opportunities to broaden and replenish our repertoire of planning and teaching strategies. The enormous variety of methods and curricula that are available support a wide range of individual teaching styles: we can select those techniques and ideas that work best for us, grafting them onto our tried-and-true routines to create a more effective approach to supporting our students' learning.

On the other hand, some of these "new" ideas look suspiciously like the ones that have gone before. Sorting through this plethora of old and new teaching practices can be time-consuming, baffling, and annoying. How can we tell, amid the shifting labels and thickets of terminology, what the significant similarities and differences are between what we are already doing and other approaches? How can we fit the various pieces together in a sensible way?

Comparing the Framework to Other Teaching Strategies

The following section is designed to respond to some of these questions by briefly comparing and contrasting the Teaching for Understanding Framework with other popular teaching and learning ideas, both old and new.

Back to Basics

Such performances of understanding as explaining, giving examples, and so on certainly are basic intellectual skills in some sense. But "back to basics" usually means something more like emphasizing the routine, basic skills of reading, writing, and arithmetic. These kinds of basic skills are also integral to teaching for understanding. However, in a classroom that puts understanding up front, these skills are taught within the context of more complex performances of understanding. For instance, students learn about using decimal points by calculating interest on a loan or a savings account. They learn to write complete sentences as they create books of short stories for younger students. In this way students learn not only the skills, but also why they are important and how to apply them effectively.

Of course, students need repeated opportunities to practice and refine some skills. These skills are best developed over the course of several units—or even in every unit—throughout the course or year. Focused practice sessions can also be useful if students understand the relationship between the skill they are practicing and the performance (or performances) of understanding in which they will use the skill.

Cooperative Learning

Many performances of understanding can involve cooperative learning—for instance, students working in teams to prepare for and carry out a debate. Asking students during the ongoing assessment process to give one another feedback on their work is another way in which cooperative learning can play a role in this approach to teaching for understanding. However, cooperative learning in and of itself is not the same thing as teaching for understanding. Indeed, there are many applications of cooperative learning—such as placing students in teams so that they can help one another memorize the definitions of vocabulary words—that have nothing to do with fostering understanding. (However, if group work is appropriately supported with well-defined goals and ongoing assessment, it might help students develop their understanding of the processes and challenges of teamwork.)

Essential Questions

An essential question, as conceived by the Coalition of Essential Schools, is a question that captures the most important aspects of a topic that students study during a given unit. As such it embodies aspects of both generative topics and understanding goals (both unit-long and overarching). Essential questions, like generative topics and understanding goals, designate the "what" of the curriculum and demand that that "what" be important, engaging, and related to students' lives. Some teachers who have worked with both the Teaching for Understanding Framework and the Coalition's idea of essential questions have related the two in this way: a generative topic is a broad field for exploration (say, "The Civil War"); essential questions direct students to consider particular aspects of that topic ("Is the Civil War still going on today?"); and unit-long understanding goals spell out what students need to understand in order to respond effectively to the question ("Students will develop their understanding of the various issues and concerns that led to the Civil War, the degree to which those issues were addressed during the post–Civil War era, and the ways in which those issues are addressed or go unresolved in today's society"). Essential questions that guide an entire course rather than a single unit are equivalent to the question form of overarching understanding goals or throughlines. Because essential questions already pose questions for students to address, teachers who work with both essential questions and unit-level understanding goals usually phrase the goals as statements only (rather than both as questions and as statements).

Exhibitions

The concept of exhibitions is another Coalition of Essential Schools idea that is congenial to the Teaching for Understanding Framework. An exhibition is a complex, culminating performance of understanding that requires students to integrate a number of skills and understandings. But unlike performances of understanding, exhibitions are by definition public and include feedback not only from teachers and classmates but also from persons outside the school—professionals from the community, parents, and so on. Some teachers who have combined the concept of exhibitions with that of understanding performances have designed units around a series of introductory and guided inquiry performances of understanding that lead up to an exhibition (which stands as the culminating performance of understanding) in which students draw together the understandings they developed in the previous performances. True to the concept of exhibitions, this final performance of understanding is often presented formally to an audience that includes community members as well as classmates and is evaluated by judges other than the teacher.

Hands-On Learning

Many (though not all) performances of understanding are hands-on activities. Not all hands-on activities are performances of understanding, however. What makes the difference? The degree to which the activity leads students to use what they know in new ways determines whether it is an understanding performance. For example, in a science unit on aerodynamics students might build and fly kites. This is a good hands-on activity, but it is not necessarily a performance of understanding. Students could, for example, follow the instructions on a kite kit and produce a kite that flies, without ever developing an understanding of aerodynamic design. The activity would become a performance of understanding only if the students were asked to explain why some kites fly better than others, or to make incremental changes to the design of their kites and predict the effect the changes will have on the kites' flight patterns, or to apply the principles of kite design to that of planes in order to explain how planes fly. Engaging students' hands is not enough: to be a performance of understanding, an activity must present a cognitive challenge that will lead students to develop and demonstrate understanding.

Interdisciplinary Curricula

Many generative topics lend themselves to interdisciplinary study—that is, they offer opportunities for content and methodology from two or more disciplines to be brought together in the process of addressing a particular issue or problem. One advantage of focusing on the interdisciplinary aspects of a topic is that it makes the connections between that topic and other areas (one of the criteria for generative topics) more apparent. However, generative topics do not have to be approached in an interdisciplinary way. Because many connections can be made between issues within a single discipline, one can teach for understanding just as effectively by focusing on a single discipline or domain.

Lectures

Students need new information if they are to engage in understanding performances for new topics. Lectures are a perfectly legitimate mode of providing information. However, the information provided in lectures needs to serve directly the understanding goals for the unit and the performances of understanding in which the students are engaged. Teachers who have used the Teaching for Understanding Framework have found that lectures work best when they are brief, targeted, and given in response to questions students raise as they carry out performances of understanding.

Multiple Intelligences–Based Teaching

Good performances of understanding (or good combinations of performances) allow students to build and demonstrate understanding in a variety of ways. Designing performances with an eye toward supporting students' multiple intelligences is one way to allow for this variety. All performances, however, should help students develop the understandings stated in the understanding goals. For instance, if you want your students to develop their grasp of the interrelatedness of all living things, you might ask them to write an essay explaining what effects a new town dump would have if it were placed in territory frequented by the area's red fox population (a traditional, linguistic-based performance). You might also ask them to draw a chart showing the effects of this interruption in the food chain (a task that draws on spatial ability). And you might ask them to role-play what they would say to particular town council members to persuade them to put the dump elsewhere (a performance that draws on interpersonal as well as linguistic intelligence). You would not ask students simply to draw a picture of the proposed location of the town dump or to write a song about red foxes, however. While both of these tasks would allow students to use different intelligences, neither would encourage them to grapple with their understanding of interrelatedness.

Portfolios

Portfolios, in which students collect their work over long periods of time, can be a valuable tool in teaching and learning for understanding. They can facilitate ongoing assessment, enabling you and your students to review their progress toward the understanding goals by looking at the development of their work over time. For example, some teachers ask their students to review their portfolios at certain points during the year and select pieces of work that demonstrate their growing understanding of a throughline or a unit-long understanding goal. Asking students to write a reflective piece explaining their selections provides teachers, parents, and the students themselves with valuable information about the students' understanding. As tools for such ongoing assessment, portfolios that include examples from all phases of students' work (initial and interim drafts as well as the final products) are often more helpful than portfolios containing only selected "best works."

Project-Based Learning

Many performances of understanding are projectlike: they are relatively complex, long-term, and problem-focused. However, projects can be impressive and eye-catching without really fostering understanding. In teaching for understanding, projects must help students achieve the understanding goals, and they must be accompanied by ongoing assessment in which students and the teacher reflect on and provide feedback about the work.

At the same time, it is important to recognize that performances of understanding do not have to be projects: there are many nonproject performances (such as students' explaining a concept in their own words or comparing and contrasting two sides of a controversial issue) that can help students develop their understanding.

Textbook-Based Teaching

Textbooks are one way of providing students with the information they need to carry out new performances of understanding. However, textbooks present difficulties on several levels with regard to teaching for understanding. Often they do not provide the kind of new information that serves understanding goals and performances well. Instead they contain bare facts that are hard for students to summarize and explain (to name two understanding performances), or they highlight abstract principles that are hard for students to exemplify or apply (two more examples of performances of understanding).

Although solving textbook problems or responding to textbook questions can be performances of understanding (depending on how much they ask students to stretch their thinking), they are only one kind of performance. Students who solve textbook problems using Newton's laws typically do not also explain them in their own words, find fresh examples of them (examples abound in everyday life), think about how to test them, and so on. Conventional problem solving, challenging though it often is, involves too narrow a range of understanding performances to build understanding.

Finally, while many textbooks are organized according to theme or topic, those themes and topics are not necessarily generative. Textbooks can be a good starting place for gathering ideas for generative topics, but generally their topics need to be culled and revised in order to allow more room for the particular interests and experiences of your students. Textbooks can be one support in the process of helping your students achieve the understanding goals you have established, but they should not be the only one.

Thinking Skills Curricula

Thinking skills curricula can provide useful supports to help you design performances of understanding and help your students carry them out. Most full-fledged performances of understanding require some kind of high-level thinking such as causal reasoning, justification, problem finding, problem solving, decision making, or exploring multiple perspectives and points of view. Thinking skills curricula can help you identify and support the kinds of thinking skills you want your students to develop and use in the context of their performances of understanding. Conversely, knowing more specifically the kinds of thinking you want your students to be able to do can help you in constructing performances of understanding that will give them opportunities to do it.

As with other basic skills, thinking skills need to be developed in the context of performances of understanding. Periodic focused practice sessions may help students develop specific thinking skills; however, students need to see the connection between these practice sessions and the performances of understanding in which the thinking skills in question will be used.

REFLECTION

As you think about important approaches, ideas, and techniques you have incorporated into your practice, you may find it useful to write about or discuss the following questions:

> *In what ways does the Teaching for Understanding Framework capture similar ideas? What aspects of the framework might complement or reshape the other components of your practice?*

> *What do the other important techniques or approaches in your practice offer that the Teaching for Understanding Framework does not? How might the two be combined? (You might try diagraming this relationship.)*

Glossary of Terms

Generative Topics

Those topics, issues, themes, concepts, ideas, and so on that provide enough depth, significance, connections, and variety of perspective to support students' development of powerful understandings. Typically they are interesting to students and teachers, central to one or more domains or disciplines, and accessible to students. See page 30 for examples.

Ongoing Assessment

The continual process of providing students with clear responses to their work that will help them improve their performances of understanding. The ongoing assessment process tells teachers and students about what the student understands *and* about how to proceed with subsequent teaching and learning. The process requires two conditions: (1) that performances of understanding have clear, public assessment criteria that are closely related to the understanding goals and (2) that students have the opportunity to receive feedback about their performances of understanding both during and after the performance (thus enabling them to use the feedback to improve their work). See pages 80–83 for examples.

Overarching Understanding Goals

Goals that identify the concepts, processes, and skills about which we want students to develop understanding throughout an entire course. Overarching understanding goals span generative topics: they can be addressed in the context of virtually every generative topic taught during a course. Typically, unit-long understanding goals are more specific versions of the overarching understanding goals. Also known as "throughlines." See page 45 for examples.

Performances of Understanding

Activities that require students to use knowledge in new ways or situations. In such activities students reshape, expand on, extrapolate from, apply, and build on what they already know. Performances of understanding help students to build as well as demonstrate their understanding. Also known as "understanding performances." See pages 63–65 for examples.

Throughlines

Goals that identify the concepts, processes, and skills about which we want students to develop understanding. Throughlines span generative topics: they can be addressed in the context of virtually every generative topic taught during a course. Typically, unit-long understanding goals are more specific versions of the throughlines for a course. Also known as "overarching understanding goals." See page 45 for examples.

Understanding Goals

Goals that identify the concepts, processes, and skills about which we want students to develop understanding. They are worded in two ways: as statements (that can begin, "Students will understand . . ." or "Students will appreciate . . ." or "Students will develop their understanding of . . .") and as open-ended questions. There are two "sizes" of understanding goals: "unit-long" understanding goals, which are fairly specific and pertain to a particular period of instruction, and "overarching" understanding goals (or "throughlines"), which pertain to an entire course or year. See pages 44–45 for examples.

Understanding Performances

Activities that require students to use knowledge in new ways or situations. In such activities students reshape, expand on, extrapolate from, apply, and build on what they already know. Understanding performances help students to build as well as demonstrate their understanding. Also known as "performances of understanding." See pages 63–65 for examples.

Unit-Long Understanding Goals

Goals that identify the concepts, processes, and skills about which we want students to develop understanding during a particular curriculum unit. Unit-long understanding goals are closely related to the overarching understanding goals, or throughlines, for the course. See pages 44–45 for examples.